STUDENT BOOK

¿Amazing English!™

AN INTEGRATED ESL CURRICULUM

Michael Walker

▲▼ Addison-Wesley Publishing Company

ISBN 0-201-85377-9 Softbound
3 4 5 6 7 8 9 10-BAM-00 99 98 97

ISBN 0-201-59978-3 Hardbound
2 3 4 5 6 7 8 9 10-BAM-00 99 98 97

CONTENTS

We Work and Play

*Work with your partner. Take turns asking for
directions and giving directions "to" and "from."*

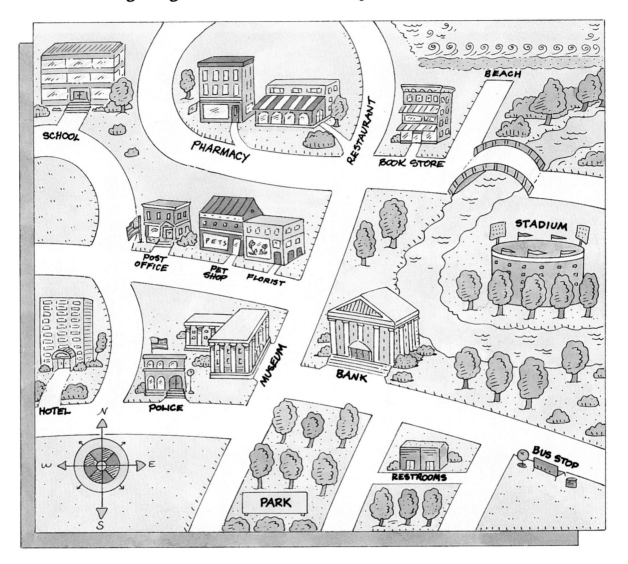

DATA BANK

1. From the hotel to the bookstore.
2. From the post office to the bus stop.
3. From the pharmacy to the bank.
4. From the bus stop to the police station.
5. From the school to the museum.
6. From the bridge to the restrooms.
7. From the florist to the park.
8. From the beach to the hotel.

P**ROBLEM** S**OLVING**

You can talk this problem over with your partner or you can work alone.

 Mrs. Comb  Miss Bunn  Mr. Pill  Mr. Apple  Miss Rose

There are five small businesses on Main Street. The business owners are: Mrs. Comb, who is not the hairdresser, Miss Bunn, who is not the baker, Mr. Pill, who is not the pharmacist, Mr. Apple who is not the grocer, and Miss Rose, who is not the florist.

Miss Rose owns a business on the end. Mr. Pill's business is the next to the grocer's. He's very friendly with the baker. He hopes she will sell him her business one day.

Who owns each business?

leaves Miss Bunn, who must be the grocer.
isn't Miss Bunn. So it must be Mrs. Comb. Mr. Apple is not the grocer, so he must be the pharmacist. That
pharmacist, but his business is next to the grocer's. The baker is a woman. So he must be the florist. The baker is a woman, but it
Miss Rose is not the florist, but her business is on one end. So she must be the hairdresser. Mr. Pill is not the

We Work and Play

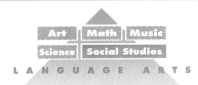

L A N G U A G E   A R T S

5

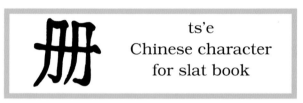

5 x 1	5
5 x 2	10
5 x 3	15
5 x 4	20
5 x 5	25
5 x 6	30
5 x 7	35
5 x 8	40
5 x 9	45
5 x 10	50

Make a Math Slat Book

Long ago in China, people made slat books out of strips of wood or bamboo strung together on cords. You can make a slat book to help you with math.

YOU WILL NEED:

- 10 craft sticks or strips of paper 3/4" x 6"
- 2 pieces of yarn or ribbon, each 28" long
- marker or pencil

册	ts'e Chinese character for slat book

1. Fold each piece of yarn in half.

2. Put a stick in the fold and tie double knots tightly against the stick. The knots must be tight because they will hold the book together.

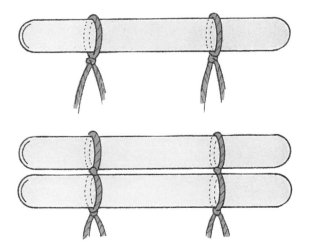

3. Put the next stick between the pieces of yarn and tie knots again.

4. Repeat until all the sticks are tied together. Use double knots after the first and last sticks. You can use single or double knots for the others.

5. Write numbers on the sticks for multiplication, addition, subtraction, or division tables.

6. Share your math slat book with friends and family.

The Boy Who Cried Wolf

Once, a shepherd boy was watching his flock of sheep. He got bored, and decided to have some fun.

"Help, help!" he cried. "Wolf! Wolf! The wolves are attacking my sheep."

The people in the village came running to help. The shepherd boy laughed and said, "There are no wolves. I was just fooling." The villagers went back to their work.

But the shepherd boy cried, "Wolf! Wolf!" three more times. Three more times, the villagers came running. And three more times the boy laughed. He thought it was a great joke. The villagers did not.

Soon after, some wolves really did come. The shepherd boy cried, "Wolf! Wolf!" But the villagers didn't come. The boy ran to the village.

"Help! The wolves are attacking my sheep!" he cried. "You won't fool us again," said the villagers. And so the boy lost all of his sheep.

Liars are not believed, even when they tell the truth.

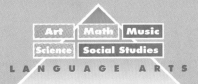

A

I, we, you, they	He, she, it
walk study	walks studies
live fix	lives fixes
play	plays

Take turns with your partner.
Ask and answer the questions.

A. 1. What do they buy? (bread)
   2. Where does he live? (Chicago)
   3. What does he like? (baseball)
   4. Where do you work? (store)

B. 1. What do they play? (football)
   2. What does she enjoy? (music)
   3. What do they say? (hello)
   4. What does he buy? (hat)

C. 1. What does he fix? (bikes)
   2. What do we brush? (teeth)
   3. What do you watch? (TV)
   4. What do you wash? (car)

D. 1. Where does the plane fly? (Miami)
   2. What do we study? (English)
   3. Where does she hurry to? (school)
   4. What do they carry? (bookbags)

AMAZING FACTS

● The smell of peppermint can make you feel more alert at school. Lavender and vanilla can make you feel more relaxed.

● Your TV picture is made up of more than 5,000 *pixels*, or dots, per square inch!

● The average human brain weighs three pounds.

On weekends, my Aunt Julie likes to drive to the mountains. She camps outdoors. Every Friday, she rushes home from work. She packs her things in a little trailer. She attaches the trailer to the back of her car. She drives up Route 93 to the mountains.

One weekend, Julie is on her way. She hears a police siren. She pulls off the highway to the side of the road. The police officer gets out of his car. Julie says, "What's wrong officer? Was I driving too fast?"

"Yes," replies the officer. "And you have two tail lights missing." Julie looks puzzled. She gets out of the car and walks to the back. She stops, throws her hands in the air, and screams! "Take it easy, lady," the officer says. "It's only a couple of tail lights."

"Tail lights? Forget the tail lights," Julie shouts. "Where's my trailer?"

Right or Wrong?

1. Julie likes to go to the beach.
2. She packs her things in the car.
3. She drives up Route 101.
4. She hears a police siren.
5. She pulls over.
6. The officer stays in his car.
7. Julie looks happy.
8. Julie's trailer is missing.

Check This Out!

THE U.S. PATENT OFFICE OPENED IN 1790.

Over 5,000,000 patents have been issued. Official patent #1 went to Samuel Hopkins for an invention that made soap. Other inventors' ideas didn't quite work out!

Rub A Dub Dub

FRANCES ALLEN'S PORTABLE BATHTUB – attach the two hoses to a water source, close the bag with an inside zipper, and lather up! When your bath was over you could drain the bag and roll it up until the next trip.

Great Escape Gear

In 1879, many tall buildings were being built. This worried Benjamin Oppenheimer. How could a person escape if a tall building caught fire? Oppenheimer invented a parachute hat and padded shoes to provide a soft landing.

WAKE UP

Samuel Applegate was always worried about oversleeping. So in 1882, he created this device. He attached 60 corks to pieces of string. All of them were hung over a bed by a cord attached to a clock. When it was time to get up, the clock released the cord. All the corks fell on the person sleeping below!

AMAZING FACTS

- Do you think it's easy to manufacture peanut butter? It takes 548 peanuts to make one jar!

- Robots are not new inventions. The Chinese people invented them over 750 years ago.

Art | Math | Music
Science | Social Studies
LANGUAGE ARTS

Young Inventors Help Others

Kids in Bothell, Washington, read about a "surf chair" that allows people in wheelchairs to go on the beach and into shallow water.

The fourth and fifth-graders in Spiritridge School decided to build an "all-terrain chair" for their classmates in wheelchairs. They called the company that made the "surf chair" for ideas. They also called wheelchair manufacturers, hardware, plumbing, motorcycle, golf, bicycle, and dune buggy stores!

First, they built a prototype out of Tinkertoys, straws, and ice-cream sticks. Next came scale drawings. Then they followed the drawings and used PVC pipe, a metal base frame, and wheelbarrow wheels. They added a beach umbrella, colorful cushions, and a shoulder harness. The wheelchair was ready to roll. Now, students who once could only watch a baseball game can wheel right up to home plate and get a hit!

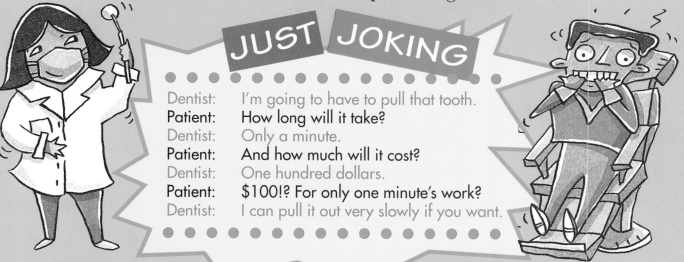

JUST JOKING

Dentist: I'm going to have to pull that tooth.
Patient: How long will it take?
Dentist: Only a minute.
Patient: And how much will it cost?
Dentist: One hundred dollars.
Patient: $100!? For only one minute's work?
Dentist: I can pull it out very slowly if you want.

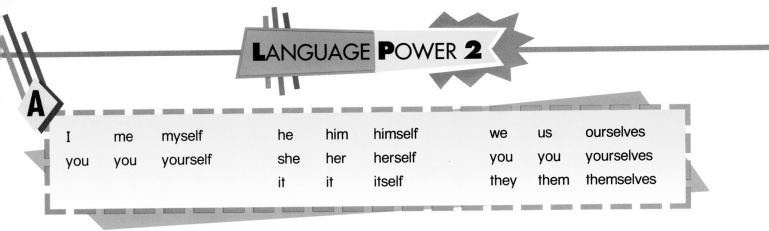

A

I	me	myself	he	him	himself		we	us	ourselves
you	you	yourself	she	her	herself		you	you	yourselves
			it	it	itself		they	them	themselves

Ask and answer questions like these with your partner.

1. ★ What's the matter with him?
   ● He hurt himself.

2. ★ Please help me.
   ● Oh, you can do it yourself.

Tom Talker was a know-it-all. He thought a lot of himself. He often said to himself, "Sometimes I'm so smart, I amaze even myself." He also thought he was handsome, and often looked at himself in the mirror.

One day, Tom saw Martha at the store. "Oh, no," Martha thought to herself. Tom walked up to her. "I'm feeling very, very smart today," he said. "Ask me anything."

"Anything?" said Martha. "Hmm. Okay. I'll bet you can't answer my question." "Fine," Tom replied. "And I'll bet you can't answer my question."

"What has three legs, flies and talks to itself at night?" asked Martha.

Tom looked puzzled. Finally he said, "I give up. I don't know. What is the answer?"

Martha smiled to herself. "I don't know either. But if that's your question, I guess I win!"

1. What did Tom often say to himself?
2. What did he often do in front of the mirror?
3. What did Martha say to herself when she saw Tom?
4. What did she do?
5. How did Martha fool Tom?

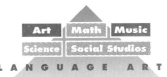

B

★ Thanks for helping Betty.
● I wasn't helping her.
★ You weren't?
● No, she did it herself.

I thought you were helping Betty, but I was wrong.

Now make conversations with your partner. Be careful!

1.
I thought you were helping Tom, but I was wrong.

2.
I thought you were helping Bill and Ted, but I was wrong.

3.
I thought you were helping Martha, but I was wrong.

4.
I thought you were helping your teacher, but I was wrong.

Practice these conversations with your partner.

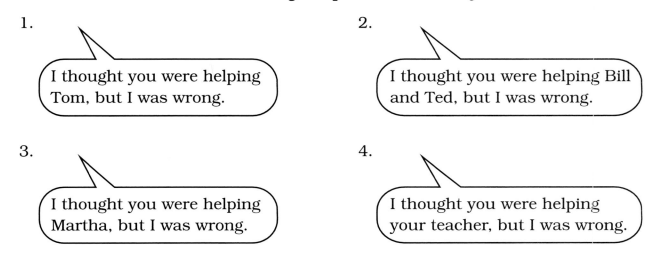

1. ★ Can you help me?
   ● Sorry, I can't help you.
      But you can do it yourself.

2. ★ Can you help us?
   ● Sorry, I can't help you.
      But you can do it yourselves.

Harry Rowland is the captain of the *Mississippi Queen*. Our ***Amazing English* Reporter** is interviewing him.

AER: Tell us about the *Mississippi Queen,* Captain.

R: Well, she's a paddle steamer. She is five decks high. There is a theater and a swimming pool on board.

AER: How many passengers can the ship take?

R: There are cabins for 400 passengers and a crew of 100.

AER: And you go up and down the Mississippi?

R: That's right.

AER: Just how long is the Mississippi?

R: It's 2,348 miles long. It begins in Lake Itasca, Minnesota. It ends in the Gulf of Mexico.

AER: Is it the longest river in North America?

R: No. The Missouri-Red Rock is longer. It flows into the Mississippi. There are more than 250 other rivers that join the Mississippi. So you can travel tens of thousands of miles and be on rivers the whole time.

AER: Well, thank you, Captain. This was a very interesting interview.

R: You're welcome.

Art | Math | Music
Science | Social Studies
LANGUAGE ARTS

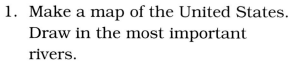
1. Make a map of the United States. Draw in the most important rivers.
   Draw in the largest lakes.
   Draw in mountains and deserts.
   Mark with a circle some important cities.

2. Now you have a map, but you have no labels for the map. Instead of writing labels, put numbers next to each thing drawn. Then make a number card for each number on your map. Put the number cards in a box. Make a list of the numbers and the names they stand for. Refer to the list when you need to check the right answer.

Play a game with a partner. Exchange maps and number cards. Take turns pulling out number cards. Find the same number on the map and name the place to win a point. Another way you can play is like this:

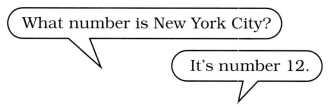

What number is New York City?

It's number 12.

3. At home, make a new map of another country or make another map of the United States. Play a map game with your family. Keep adding numbers to your first map, and soon you'll be an expert at geography!

Dear Themework,

I now have 78 numbers on my map! I have all the states, but I can't remember all of them yet. My brother is crazy about football. He has all of his favorite teams on his map. My friend Marco has a map of the ports along the Mississippi. Anna has a map of California. She has over 20 cities and towns. She even has highways numbered on her map! We all like adding numbers and playing the game.

Sincerely yours,
Janice Jackson

Liu-Always-In-A-Hurry

A FOLKTALE FROM CHINA

In China long ago, there was a farmer named Liu. He was not a patient man. He was very impatient. He was always in a hurry. He rushed through breakfast. He rushed through lunch. He rushed through his work. He wanted to be first in everything. He didn't worry about being careful in his work. He just wanted to finish it quickly.

One day, Liu was in the village. Some farmers were talking about their rice.

"My rice is doing very well," said one farmer. "It is almost three inches high."

"My rice is already three inches high," said another farmer.

Liu hurried home. He measured his rice. The plants were strong and healthy. But they were only two inches high.

Liu decided to hurry his plants along. He pulled each plant up from the ground until it was over three inches high. "Now my rice is higher than anyone's," he thought. "Tomorrow it will be even higher!"

The next morning, Liu hurried out to his rice field. The little rice plants were dead.

The people of the village soon heard about Liu's rice. They laughed and shook their heads. They said, "Foolish Liu-always-in-a-hurry! That's what happens when you don't have any patience."

This story happened long ago. But today in China, people have a saying for someone who is not patient or careful:

Don't be a rice-puller!

George Washington Carver

●●●●●●●●●●●●●●●●●●●●●●●

Here is a picture of George Washington Carver. You will hear about his life and work as you listen to the story.

▶ LISTEN

Listen to the beginning of the story. Then answer the questions.

1. Why was George Washington Carver a slave?
   a. His mother was a slave.
   b. He was born in Missouri.
   c. The Civil War was starting.

2. How did George learn to read and write?
   a. He became free after the Civil War.
   b. Moses Carver's wife taught him.
   c. He went to school when he was fourteen.

3. How did George get the money to go to college?
   a. He took the name George Carver.
   b. He earned money by doing many different jobs.
   c. People gave him the money he needed.

4. What did George concentrate on in the greenhouse?
   a. He was in charge of the greenhouse.
   b. He concentrated on vegetables and flowers.
   c. He concentrated on the peanut.

▶ SPEAK

Tell about what has happened so far. Name some peanut products you know about.

Self Holistic Portfolio
Traditional Performance
A S S E S S M E N T

▶ READ

Two years later, a famous black educator named Booker T. Washington offered George a job. The job was at a new college for black students in Tuskeegee, Alabama. The job was teaching agriculture.

Almost all the students were sons and daughters of poor farmers. The farmers were still growing cotton. Cotton was the crop they had always grown – since the time they were slaves. George tried to teach the children of these farmers how to grow peanuts. Cotton robbed the soil of food. Peanuts didn't. Peanuts put food back into the soil. Little by little, farmers began to grow peanuts.

George Washington Carver continued to study and research uses of the peanut. He spent the rest of his life at Tuskeegee Institute. He helped poor farmers improve their land. He helped them to change from growing only cotton. He never became rich; he never became really famous. But he helped change a whole way of life in the American South. George Washington Carver died in 1943.

The work of George Washington Carver lives on. Today, peanuts and by-products of peanuts are used to make many, many things.

▶ WRITE
How did George Washington Carver help change the way of life in the South?

▶ THINK
Why do you think George Washington Carver's work was important?

AMAZING FACTS

EACH SQUARE =
5 POINTS

THREE IN A ROW =
10 BONUS POINTS

1 What is the longest river in North America?

2 What did the farmers in Liu's village grow in their fields?

3 What crop in the South robbed the soil of food?

4 Why did Liu pull up his rice plants?

5 At what school did George Washington Carver work for most of his life?

6 What is the *Mississippi Queen*?

7 What special chair did the kids in Bothell, Washington, build?

8 What country is the math slat book from?

9 How many miles long is the Mississippi River?

Self Test Prep Portfolio
Traditional Performance
A S S E S S M E N T

Family Memories

Mexican Yarn Paintings

Family Facts

HOUSE RULES

Family Pictures

Art | Math | Music
Science | Social Studies

LANGUAGE ARTS

My Aunt Edna Eagle is a pilot. She works for the Coast Guard. She flies a helicopter. When the weather is bad, she's on alert for an emergency. Last week, she told me this story.

On Saturday, I was on patrol. The weather was foggy and cold. I knew that five ships were in port. I flew over the harbor. I could see five ships below. Every ship had two lights.

On the left, the lights were red, like this:

On the right, the lights were green, like this:

All the ships were moving slowly at about the same speed. I saw that two ships were going to crash. There was nothing I could do.

Which two ships crashed?

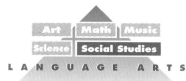

Ships C and D crashed. Only two ships were heading directly for each other. Red is left; green is right. The ships were moving like this:

Family Memories

LANGUAGE ARTS

Make a Yarn-Painting Bowl

The Huichol Indians of northwest Mexico make yarn paintings with brilliant colors and interesting designs. The paintings tell stories about their families, their history, and their religion. They press the yarn into beeswax that has been warmed by the sun, but you can use glue instead.

YOU WILL NEED:
- **yarn—many colors and lengths**
- **a paper bowl**
- **glue, popsicle stick, tape, pencil**
- **scrap cardboard**

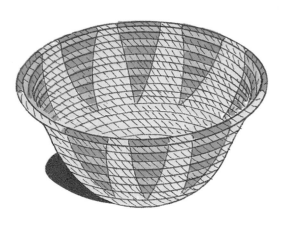

Finished bowl

1. Swirl the glue on the inside bottom of the paper bowl.

2. Take the end of a length of yarn and begin wrapping it in a circular pattern.

3. Use the popsicle stick to pat the yarn in place.

4. Keep changing colors and lengths of yarn until you reach the rim of the bowl. Be patient!

5. Flip the bowl over and repeat steps 1–4 on the outside of the bowl.

6. Take your bowl home to share with your family.

Bed in Summer

In winter I get up at night
And dress by yellow candlelight.
In summer, quite the other way,
I have to go to bed by day.

I have to go to bed and see
The birds still hopping on the trees,
Or hear the grown-up people's feet
Still going past me in the street.

And does it not seem hard to you,
When all the sky is clear and blue,
And I should like so much to play,
To have to go to bed by day?

Robert Louis Stevenson

A

fast	hot	funny	boring	good
faster	hotter	funnier	more boring	better
fastest	hottest	funniest	most boring	best
slow	sad	silly	delicious	bad
slower	sadder	sillier	more delicious	worse
slowest	saddest	silliest	most delicious	worst
big	happy	exciting		
bigger	happier	more exciting		
biggest	happiest	most exciting		

Practice conversations like these with your partner.

1. ★ Is your bike fast?
   ● Yes, it is.
   ★ Is it faster than my bike?
   ● Yes! It's the fastest bike in the world!

2. ★ Is your brother silly?
   ● Yes, he is.
   ★ Is he sillier than my brother?
   ● Yes. He's the silliest brother in the world!

3. ★ Is your book exciting?
   ● Yes, it is.
   ★ Is it more exciting than my book?
   ● Yes! It's the most exciting book in the world!

AMAZING FACTS

● The biggest family on record is a family with 69 brothers and sisters.

● What's your favorite family TV program? The oldest children's TV show is "Howdy Doody." It began in 1947.

My Uncle Jerry loves to tell stories. He says this is a true story! Uncle Jerry was on vacation. He felt very happy. He rented the smallest, cheapest car he could find. He started driving on the highway, but he didn't like it. "This is the straightest, most boring road in the world," he thought to himself.

So he drove off the highway. He found a narrow, curving road. "This is better," he thought. He drove through pretty villages. "These are the prettiest villages in the world," he thought. He stopped and talked to the friendly people. "These are the friendliest people in the world," he thought. The road became narrower and slower. Jerry felt happier and happier.

Suddenly a huge truck came around a curve. The driver leaned out of the window and shouted, "PIG!" Jerry couldn't have been more surprised. "That's the unfriendliest person in the world," he thought. "And PIG to you," he shouted back. He drove around the curve. He slammed on his brakes. In the middle of the road was the biggest pig in the world!

1. What kind of car did Jerry rent?
2. Why didn't he like the highway?
3. What kind of road did he find?
4. How did he feel?
5. What did he think about the villages?
6. What did he think about the people?
7. What did he think about the driver?
8. What was in the middle of the road?

Animal Families

HERE ARE SOME NAMES OF ANIMALS AND ANIMAL GROUPS.
CAN YOU MATCH THEM CORRECTLY?

GORILLAS   CHICKS   WHALES   KANGAROOS   LIONS   BEARS   MONKEYS   TOADS

a mob of.......... a brood of........ a band of......... a troop of.........
a sleuth of........ a knot of .... a gam of .... a pride of.........

HOUSE RULES

Suppose you could make all the rules for the adults in your family. Here's what a few kids said. Make up your own rules and compare them with your friends' rules.

"My parents could only watch TV at 6:30 a.m. They would have to eat carrots every day, and they would have to take care of my little brother forever."
Meg Sullivan

"They would have to clean their room every day. And they would have to let me pick out their clothes."
Pete Peterson

"My Mom would have to walk around the block 45 times with the dog every day! And she would have to do the dishes alone."

Brad Howse

AMAZING FACTS

- The average grown-up watches TV about four hours a day. The average kid watches TV six and a half hours a day!

- 160 babies are born every minute!

- Even identical twins aren't exactly alike: their fingerprints are different.

Boy or Girl?

If an alligator's eggs are kept at a temperature of 86 degrees or less, all the babies will be sisters. At higher temperatures, all the babies will be brothers!

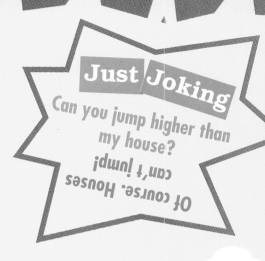

Just Joking

Can you jump higher than my house?

Of course. Houses can't jump!

The First Airplane Flight

Orville and Wilbur Wright invented the first successful airplane. The two brothers flipped a coin to see who got to test fly it first.

Orville took their plane, named "Flyer 1," up in the air in 1903. It flew for 12 seconds. Orville had to lie down to fly the plane. He balanced it by moving his hips.

Wilbur took the plane up on the fourth flight of the day. It stayed in the air for 59 seconds. But wind knocked it over and wrecked it after landing.

It was the last flight of "Flyer 1."

Go for it, Bro!

A

hear	hears	heard	take	takes	took
see	sees	saw	come	comes	came
run	runs	ran	tell	tells	told
drive	drives	drove	stand	stands	stood
say	says	said	bring	brings	brought

This is another story from Uncle Jerry.

It was a quiet day. Suddenly a police officer heard a scream. She ran around the corner. She couldn't believe her eyes. There was a man with a huge lion on a leash. "Hey, you!" she said. "You can't walk around the streets with a lion. Take it to the zoo!"

"Okay, officer. I just wanted to show Baby the town." The man opened the door of his car and the lion jumped in. The officer stood and stared as the man drove off in the direction of the zoo.

The next day, the police officer saw the same man and the same lion again. "Hey you!" she said. "Come over here! And bring that lion with you!" The man brought the lion over to the officer.

"What's the problem, officer?" "Problem? I told you yesterday to take that lion to the zoo!"

"Oh, I did officer. I took Baby to the zoo. He enjoyed it very much. But today, I'm taking him to the movies!"

Take turns with your partner. Read the sentences aloud and choose the right form of the verb.

1. ★ Do you think she is nice?
   ● Yes, I (think, thinks) she is very nice.

2. ★ What kind of car do they drive?
   ● They (drive, drives) a van.

3. ★ What does he take to school?
   ● He (takes, take) the bus.

4. ★ Where does she run?
   ● She (run, runs) in the park.

5. We (bring, brings) our lunch to school.

1. ★ Do you think she is nice?
   ● Yes, I (think, thinks) she is very nice.

2. ★ What kind of car do they drive?
   ● They (drive, drives) a van.

3. ★ What does he take to school?
   ● He (takes, take) the bus.

4. ★ Where does she run?
   ● She (run, runs) in the park.

5. We (bring, brings) our lunch to school.
6. He (says, say) hello.
7. They (stands, stand) in line.
8. I (hear, hears) the bell.
9. (Do, Does) you like milk?
10. (Do, Does) she feel happy?
11. We (don't, doesn't) like eggs.
12. (Don't, Doesn't) he eat meat?
13. I (don't, doesn't) drive a car.
14. They (do, does) like eggs.

Trevor Tyler is a historian. He studies families and cultures around the world. He has spent many years studying the Maori natives of New Zealand. Our *Amazing English* **Reporter** is interviewing him.

AER: How far back do the Maori in New Zealand go?

T: Well, they arrived some time in the fourteenth century.

AER: What sort of people were they?

T: They were fighters, mainly. They were very brave. There's a story— we don't know if it's true or not.

But there's a story about the Maori fighting Captain Cook. When Cook and his men were just about beaten, the Maori sent food to them so they could fight longer!

AER: Was the land and climate the same then?

T: Yes, it was. The earliest settlers of New Zealand found a subtropical climate. They found beautiful mountains, lakes, forests, and fiords.

AER: How did the Maori live?

T: They lived in villages. There was always a fortress near each village. They called it a "Pa." Each group had its own chief.

AER: Didn't they have a lot of gods?

T: Yes. The most powerful god was called Io. The Maoris also believed in the laws of Tapu. Tapu protected the chief and the lands of the tribe. If you broke the Tapu, they believed you'd be punished.

AER: Tapu?

T: Yes, that's right. It's the same as the English word *taboo*, which means something forbidden.

Art | Math | Music
Science | Social Studies
L A N G U A G E   A R T S

1. Work with a partner. Find out more about the Maori of New Zealand. Compare their lives in the past and in the present. Is the Maori story at all like the story of Native Americans?

2. There are many English-speaking countries today, such as Canada, Australia, Belize and New Zealand. Choose one country to research. Was it once a colony? How did it get its independence? Where did the colonial settlers come from? How did the new settlers change the lives of the natives? What is life like in that country today?

3. Captain Cook was a famous English explorer. Choose one explorer to research. Find out as much as you can about this person. Was he/she famous before death?

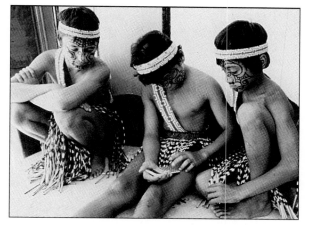

Maori boys in traditional dress discover the wonders of a calculator.

Dear Themework,
I didn't really know anything about Canada until this project. But Canada is a neighbor! People in Canada speak English (and French). The way they live sure looks like the way people in the U.S. live. My family is planning a trip to Nova Scotia. People call it Canada's Ocean Playground. After our vacation, I'll do a report on this province.

Yours,
Jimmy Gibbs

Family Pictures

EXCERPTED FROM THE BOOK BY CARMEN LOMAS GARZA

The pictures in this book are all painted from my memories of growing up in Kingsville, Texas, near the border with Mexico.

Carmen Lomas Garza

Art | Math | Music
Science | Social Studies

LANGUAGE ARTS

MAKING TAMALES

This is a scene from my parents' kitchen. Everybody is making tamales. My grandfather is wearing blue overalls and a blue shirt. I'm right next to him with my sister Margie. We're helping to soak the dried leaves from the corn. My mother is spreading the cornmeal dough on the leaves and my aunt and uncle are spreading meat on the dough. My grandmother is lining up the rolled and folded tamales ready for cooking. In some families just the women make tamales, but in our family everybody helps.

WATERMELON

It's a hot summer evening. The whole family's on the front porch. My grandfather had brought us some watermelons that afternoon. We put them in the refrigerator and let them chill down. After supper we went out to the front porch. My father cut the watermelon and gave each one of us a slice.

It was fun to sit out there. The light was so bright on the porch that you couldn't see beyond the edge of the lit area. It was like being in our own little world.

ORANGES

We were always going to my grandparents' house, so whatever they were involved in we would get involved in. In this picture my grandmother is hanging up the laundry. We told her that the oranges needed picking so she said, "Well, go ahead and pick some." Before she knew it, she had too many oranges to hold in her hands, so she made a basket out of her apron. That's my brother up in the tree, picking oranges. The rest of us are picking up the ones that he dropped on the ground.

THE FAIR IN REYNOSA

My friends and I once went to a very big fair across the border in Reynosa, Mexico. The fair lasted a whole week. Artisans and entertainers came from all over Mexico. There were lots of booths with food and crafts. This is one little section where everybody is ordering and eating tacos.

I painted a father buying tacos and the rest of the family sitting down at the table. The little girl is the father's favorite and that's why she gets to tag along with him. I can always recognize little girls who are their fathers' favorites.

CAKEWALK

Cakewalk was a game to raise money to send Mexican Americans to the university. You paid 25 cents to stand on a number. When the music started, you walked around and around. When the music stopped, whatever number you happened to step on was your number. Then one of the ladies in the center would pick out a number from the can. If you were standing on the winning number, you would win a cake. That's my mother in the center of the circle in the pink and black dress. My father is serving punch. I'm the little girl in front of the store scribbling on the sidewalk with a twig.

Swiss Family Robinson Adventure

The *Swiss Family Robinson* is a famous book. Here is one of the family's adventures when a storm blows up at sea.

▶ LISTEN

Listen to the beginning of the story. Then answer the questions.

1. Why was the Robinson family in danger?
   a. They were lost.
   b. They were in a storm at sea.
   c. Their ship turned upside-down.

2. Why did the ship begin to sink?
   a. The sails were too heavy.
   b. There were too many people on the ship.
   c. The ship crashed into some rocks.

3. How did the Robinson family get to the island?
   a. They built a boat and sailed to the island.
   b. A plane took them to the island.
   c. They swam to the island.

4. What did the Robinson family find on the island?
   a. They found wild animals.
   b. They found food and tall trees.
   c. They found friendly people.

▶ SPEAK

Tell about what has happened so far. Who is telling the story? What animals do you think the Robinson family will find on the island? What will happen to the rest of the ship?

▶ READ

And so, we were safe and sound in our treehouse. We decided to name our island New Switzerland, after our homeland. Weeks and months passed. We discovered many things. My wife and my sons, Fritz, Ernest, Jack and Francis, spent many days exploring. We caught and tamed a wild buffalo and an eagle. My wife found some unusual berries. They were sticky. She put them in a pot and melted them. Then she made candles from the juice.

We kept taking things from the wreck. We found two small cannons. We floated them to shore. We put them on a hill to protect our treehouse.

After some months, there was nothing left on the wreck of our ship. We decided to blow it up. We hoped the wood from the ship would float ashore. My sons and I rolled a barrel of gunpowder into the bottom of the ship. We made a very long fuse. We lit it and left the ship. We got back to our island. There was a huge explosion. The wreck was gone.

▶ WRITE

After the wreck was gone, what do you think happened to the Robinson family? Make up your own ending to the story.

▶ THINK

Why was the Robinson family able to survive on the island?

AMAZING FACTS

1

What does the word *taboo* mean?

2

What is one ingredient of tamales?

3

What famous explorer went to New Zealand?

4

What are whale families called?

5

Where do the Huichol Indians live?

6

What did the Robinson family use to blow up their ship?

7

What is the cakewalk?

8

What are the natives of New Zealand called?

9

Who invented the first successful airplane?

44

Self Test Prep Portfolio
Traditional Performance
ASSESSMENT

Theme 2

That's Amazing!

Lunch Bag Tricks

AMAZING Jim Abbott

RUBE GOLDBERG INVENTION

Hot Hot Peppers

Good telephone manners are not amazing. They are required.

Hello?

Hello, is Andy there? This is Rosa.

I'm sorry, Rosa. He's not at home.

Will you ask him to call me?

Certainly. What's your number?

It's 944-3700.

944-3700. I'll give him the message.

Thanks. Bye.

Good morning. State Bank. Can I help you?

Mr. Rogers, please.

That line is busy. Will you hold?

No, I'll call back later.

DATA BANK

Operator.
Can I help you?
That line is busy.
Will you hold?

area code
information
Dial. . .

Is Pam there?
Can I speak to Pam?
Is Pam home?

Mr. Rogers, please.

Can I leave a message?
I'll call back later.
Please have him call me.

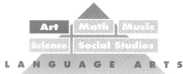

Amaze your family and friends.

A. Here is a very old game that two people can play. (It won't work if both know the secret. So after you and your partner solve this problem, you can both play with new friends.) Here are the simple rules.

Begin with number 1.
Take turns adding either 1 or 2 to your partner's number.

Player A: 1
Player B: 2 (adding 1 to 1)

Player A: 4 (adding 2 to 2)
Player B: 5 (adding 1 to 4)

The player who says the number 20 wins. Can you figure out a way to always win—no matter who begins?

B. Here's a math trick that will amaze your friends.

1. Choose a number—any number.
2. Add five.
3. Double the number.

4. Subtract four.
5. Divide by 2.
6. Subtract your first number.
7. The answer is three, right?

Start with 2, then go 5, 8, 11, 14, 17, 20. If you add 3 each time to your previous call, your opponent cannot affect the situation. He or she can only add 1 or 2 each time. If you say 2, the other person can say only 3 or 4. You say 5.

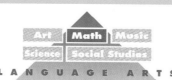

Do Amazing Lunch Bag Tricks

YOU WILL NEED:
- **plastic sandwich bags**
- **pencils**
- **a glass**
- **a rubber band**

A.

1. Fill the sandwich bag with water and knot it.

2. Hold the bag over a sink.

3. Push a pencil through one side of the bag and out the other. What happens?

4. See how many more pencils you can push through.

B.

1. Open up a sandwich bag inside a glass.

2. Push it tightly against the bottom and sides.

3. Bring the top of the bag over the rim of the glass.

4. Secure the bag with the rubber band.

5. Now reach to the bottom of the glass and try to pull the bag out of the glass.

   What happens?

The Meal

Timothy Tompkins had turnips and tea.
The turnips were tiny.
He ate at least three.
And then, for dessert,
He had onions and ice.
He liked that so much
That he ordered it twice.
He had two cups of ketchup,
A prune, and a pickle.
"Delicious," said Timothy.
"Well worth a nickel."
He folded his napkin
And hastened to add,
"It's one of the loveliest breakfasts I've had."

Karla Kuskin

Create an amazing meal of your own.

That's Amazing!

49

LANGUAGE ARTS

A

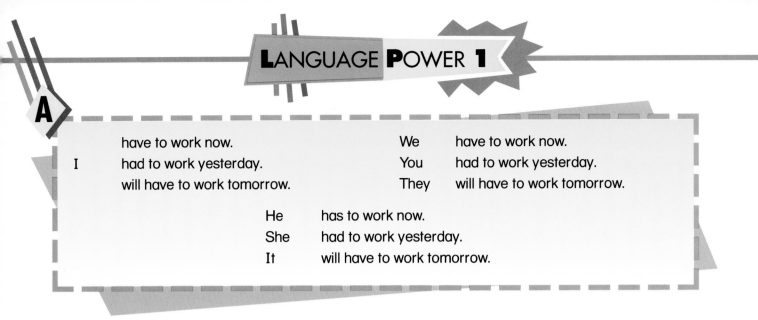

I	have to work now.		We	have to work now.
	had to work yesterday.		You	had to work yesterday.
	will have to work tomorrow.		They	will have to work tomorrow.

He	has to work now.
She	had to work yesterday.
It	will have to work tomorrow.

A clever secretary amazes, but does not amuse, the boss.

A new boss came to Ace Mattress Factory. She was very strict. She said to the secretary, "You have to keep a record of what happens every day. You have to write down everything."

The next day, the boss found a worker sleeping on a mattress. She took the worker to her office. "Write this down," she said to the secretary. "Worker was sleeping on a mattress."

"Do I have to write that?" the secretary asked.

"Yes," replied the boss, "You have to."

"But I'm a mattress tester." said the worker. "I have to rest when I test. Does he really have to write that down?"

"He has to," said the boss.

"Don't worry," said the secretary. "I just got an idea."

The next day, the boss looked at the secretary's record book. She was very angry. "What's the meaning of this?"

The secretary read from the record book: "The boss was not asleep on a mattress today." He smiled at the boss. "Well, it was true, wasn't it? So I had to write it down."

AMAZING FACTS

- A batted baseball can travel as fast as 120 miles per hour.

- An ear of corn always has an even number of rows.

- The smallest dinosaur (Compsogmathus) was only 30 inches high!

50

Art | Math | Music
Science | Social Studies

Theme 3

LANGUAGE ARTS

1. ★ I'm sorry, I can't play now.
   ● Why not?
   ★ I have to go to the dentist.

2. ★ Jack can't play today.
   ● Why not?
   ★ He has to fly to the moon!
   ● That's amazing!
   ★ Just kidding.

3. ★ I couldn't play yesterday.
   ● Why not?
   ★ I had to help my Dad.

4. ★ Jack couldn't play yesterday.
   ● Why not?
   ★ He had to interview the president.
   ● That's amazing.
   ★ Just kidding.

Work with your partner. Make conversations from the information below.

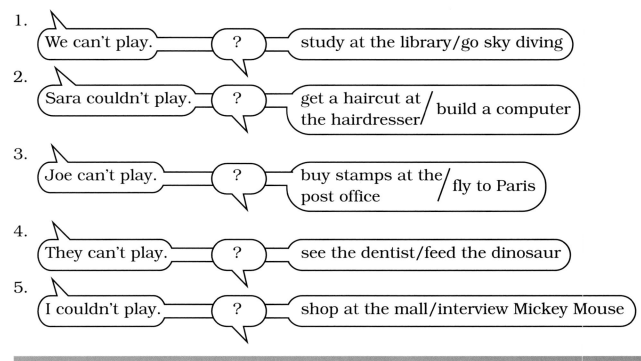

1. We can't play. ? study at the library/go sky diving

2. Sara couldn't play. ? get a haircut at the hairdresser/build a computer

3. Joe can't play. ? buy stamps at the post office/fly to Paris

4. They can't play. ? see the dentist/feed the dinosaur

5. I couldn't play. ? shop at the mall/interview Mickey Mouse

That's Amazing!

HE'S AMAZING!

JIM ABBOTT WAS BORN WITH ONLY ONE HAND. But he never let that get in the way of his dream to play professional baseball.

In order to play baseball, Jim created a special move. Reporters call it "The Amazing Abbott Switch." Jim taught himself how to switch his glove from his left hand to his right side when necessary. He does it so fast people say it looks like magic.

Jim played for the California Angels for four years. Now he is a pitcher for the New York Yankees.

Jim says, "I don't think of myself as special or great. But now I've met other kids who were also born with one hand. They tell me they won't give up on playing baseball because of me. And that's what makes me feel great!"

JUST JOKING

What does Dracula take for a cold?

COFFIN DROPS!

AMAZING FACTS

- The tiny female apple aphid can lay as many as 2100000000000000000000000000000000000000000000000000000000000000000000000000000000000000000000000000000000000000000000000 eggs in 10 months.

- An adult body is made up of 100 trillion (100,000,000,000,000) cells.

- Hummingbird eggs are smaller than jelly beans.

Crazy Machines

SCRATCH YOUR BACK? That's a simple question. Unless, of course, you asked Rube Goldberg. Rube was a newspaper cartoonist. He drew cartoons of inventions that did very simple things in a complicated and silly way. So if you have an itch, here's a Rube Goldberg invention that might help you. Notice that Rube always explains the many steps in his invention.

You try it! Use page 47 of the *Skills Journal* to create your own amazing, crazy machine.

BACK SCRATCHER

The flame from lamp (**A**) catches on curtain (**B**). Fire department shoots water (**C**) through window. Man (**D**) thinks it is raining. He reaches for umbrella (**E**), pulling string (**F**) and lifting end of platform (**G**). Iron ball (**H**) falls and pulls string (**I**), causing hammer (**J**) to hit plate of glass (**K**). Crash of glass wakes up pup (**L**). Mother dog (**M**) rocks him to sleep in cradle (**N**), causing wooden hand (**O**) to move up and down your back.

A

I have changed. But I have always had brown hair.

You have changed. But you have always had blue eyes.

He has changed. But he has always had big feet.

She has changed. But she has always had pretty hair.

We have changed. But we have always had big ears.

You two have changed. But you have always had black hair.

They have changed. But they have always had good teeth.

My, how you have changed—it's amazing!

Mario was at a party. He saw a girl across the room. He was sure she was an old friend. He walked over to her.

"Hello! It's good to see you again."

"But I. . . ."

"I'm amazed I recognized you! You have changed your hair style. You had short hair when I last saw you."

"No, I have always had long hair."

"Really? And you started wearing glasses."

"But I have always had glasses."

"And you have changed your teeth."

"No, don't be ridiculous. I have always had these teeth."

"It's good to see you, Eleanor."

"Eleanor? But my name is Jean."

"Oh, I see. Even more amazing! You have changed your name, too."

1. ★ Tom has changed, hasn't he?
   ● What do you mean?
   ★ Well, he is tall now.
   ● But Tom has always been tall.

2. ★ Frank and Jean have changed, haven't they?
   ● What do you mean?
   ★ Well, they wear glasses now.
   ● But they have always worn glasses.

Work with your partner. Make conversations from the information below.

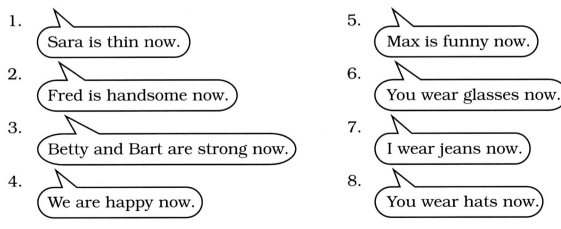

1. Sara is thin now.

2. Fred is handsome now.

3. Betty and Bart are strong now.

4. We are happy now.

5. Max is funny now.

6. You wear glasses now.

7. I wear jeans now.

8. You wear hats now.

Career Corner

Barbara Brown works at one of the biggest museums in the country. She's an expert on dinosaurs. Some people think they are the most amazing animals that ever lived. Our *Amazing English* **Reporter** is interviewing her.

AER: What sort of animals were dinosaurs?

B: They were reptiles. They were the same family as turtles, snakes, lizards, and crocodiles.

AER: Were they all the same?

B: No, there were many kinds of dinosaurs. Some were meat-eaters. Some were plant-eaters. Some walked on two legs; some walked on four legs.

AER: And they were all huge, weren't they?

B: Actually, no. Some of the first dinosaurs were no bigger than a lizard.

AER: The iguana lizard looks like a small dinosaur.

B: That's right. It does.

AER: How big were the meat-eating dinosaurs?

B: The biggest were about 90 feet long from head to tail. They had front legs that were just like short, weak arms.

AER: Unbelievable! Tell us something about the plant-eaters.

B: Some of them lived in swamps. They had long necks, but their heads were very small. Some were huge, weighing over 50 tons. That is 17 times more than a full-grown elephant weighs.

AER: Wow!

Art Math Music
Science Social Studies

LANGUAGE ARTS

1. Find out the names of five different dinosaurs. Did they walk or swim? What did they eat? Where did they live? How long ago did they live? How big were they? How long ago did they disappear?

2. Work with a partner. Make a mural or a table-top display of dinosaurs. Cut out pictures, draw, or make clay models of your favorites. Write down the information you found. Were other animals alive at the same time? If so, add them to your

project. Were people alive then? If so, tell how they lived.

3. Organize your information for an oral report. Try to answer *Who, What, Where, When, How* and *How long* questions when you present your report.

Dear Themework,
My sister and I are in the same class.
We made a huge mural. It stretched all the way around the classroom. Two friends of mine helped us too. The librarian helped us find some interesting books on flying dinosaurs. I copied out the facts and made labels for the mural. It looked really neat. We had fun making it, and we also got a good grade!

Yours truly,
Li Ann Chang

That's Amazing!

Hot, Hot, Really Hot, Red Hot Peppers

A FOLKTALE FROM KOREA

One day an old woman was in her garden. She was picking carrots and onions and cabbages and some hot, hot, really hot, RED HOT PEPPERS. Suddenly, a huge, hungry tiger came out of the forest.

"Grrrrr-ah! I'm going to eat you for lunch!" the tiger said.

"Dear me, dear me," cried the old woman. "I am too thin to make a good lunch for you. Let me eat some of my vegetables. Then I'll make a better dinner for you."

"I'll give you until midnight," the tiger said. "Then I'll be back to eat you up."

The old woman ran into her house. She cooked up a big pot of vegetables and thought about how to escape from the tiger. She sat down to eat her carrots and onions and cabbages and the hot, hot, really hot, RED HOT PEPPERS. Huge tears rolled down her cheeks. She couldn't think of a way to escape from the tiger.

Art Math Music
Science Social Studies
LANGUAGE ARTS

Then, to her surprise, a large yellow banana appeared at her door.

"Why are you crying, old woman?"

"Dear me, dear me. A tiger is coming at midnight to eat me up!"

"Oh no! Don't let the tiger get you!" said the banana. "I'll wait here by the door, just in case I can help you."

Then an enormous white egg appeared at her door.

"Why are you crying, old woman?"

"Dear me, dear me. A tiger is coming at midnight to eat me up!"

"Oh no! Don't let the tiger get you!" said the egg. "I'll wait here in the fireplace, just in case I can help you."

Soon a big brown mat appeared at her door.

"Why are you crying, old woman?"

"Dear me, dear me. A tiger is coming at midnight to eat me up!"

"Oh no! Don't let the tiger get you! said the mat. "I'll wait here in front of the fireplace, just in case I can help you."

Finally, a fat red rope appeared at her door.

"Why are you crying, old woman?"

"Dear me, dear me. A tiger is coming at midnight to eat me up!"

"Oh no! Don't let the tiger get you!" said the rope. "I'll wait here next to the mat, just in case I can help you."

The hours passed. The woman, the banana, the egg, the mat, and the rope all waited for the tiger to come back. At midnight, he did.

"Grrrah, old woman! I'm going to eat you for dinner now," the tiger growled.

"But wait," said the old woman. "Try one of my hot, hot, really hot, RED HOT PEPPERS first."

The tiger took a giant mouthful of the hot, hot, really hot, RED HOT PEPPERS.

Whooeee! The tiger's mouth was on fire! He jumped into the air and landed on the banana.

Slip. . .slap! He slipped on the banana peel and landed in the fireplace.

Blim. . .blam! The egg exploded in the tiger's face, and he jumped into the air again.

Split. . .splat! The tiger landed on the mat, and the mat rolled itself around him.

Zip. . .Zap! The rope tied itself around the mat. The old woman had escaped from the tiger after all!

The next day, seventeen soldiers came to carry the tiger away. The old woman sat at her table again. She ate a huge lunch of carrots and onions and cabbages and the hot, hot, really hot, RED HOT PEPPERS. Huge tears rolled down her cheeks again. It wasn't because she was afraid of the tiger. It was because of those hot, hot, really hot, RED HOT PEPPERS!

Alice and Humpty Dumpty

Through the Looking Glass is a famous book. This story is a conversation between two characters from that book, Alice and Humpty Dumpty.

▶ LISTEN

Listen to the beginning of the story. Then answer the questions.

1. Why did Alice think Humpty Dumpty might fall?
    a. He was standing on one leg.
    b. He was sitting on a high wall.
    c. The wall was falling down.

2. Why was Humpty Dumpty angry?
    a. Alice walked away from him.
    b. His belt fell off.
    c. Alice couldn't tell if he was wearing a necktie or a belt.

3. What is an un-birthday present?
    a. a present on a day that's not your birthday
    b. a present that isn't wrapped
    c. a present from Humpty Dumpty

4. Why is it fun to have an un-birthday?
    a. Alice will come to your party.
    b. Un-birthdays happen once a year.
    c. Un-birthdays happen many times each year.

▶ SPEAK

Tell about what has happened so far. How many days are there in a year? Do you think Humpty Dumpty likes un-birthday presents? Why?

Self Holistic Portfolio
Traditional Performance
A S S E S S M E N T

READ

> "Three hundred and sixty-five."
> "And how many birthdays do you have?"
> "One."
> "And so, there are three hundred and sixty-four days a year when you might get un-birthday presents. And only one for birthday presents!"
> Humpty Dumpty recited a poem for Alice. Then she felt she should be going.
> "Good-bye, till we meet again!" she said.
> "I wouldn't know you again if we *did* meet. You're exactly like other people."
> "Your face is the same as everybody's—two eyes, nose in the middle, mouth under. Now, if you had the two eyes on the same side of the nose, or the mouth at the top—that would be *some* help."
> "It wouldn't look very nice," Alice objected. But Humpty Dumpty only shut his eyes and said, "Wait till you've tried."
> Alice walked quietly away. She couldn't help saying to herself, "Of all the *unsatisfactory*—(She repeated this. It was a great feeling to have such a long word to say.) "Of all the unsatisfactory people I *ever* met—" She never finished the sentence. Suddenly a heavy crash shook the forest from end to end.

WRITE

What caused the crash that shook the forest? Write the next part of the story.

THINK

Why does Alice think Humpty Dumpty is an unsatisfactory person?

AMAZING FACTS

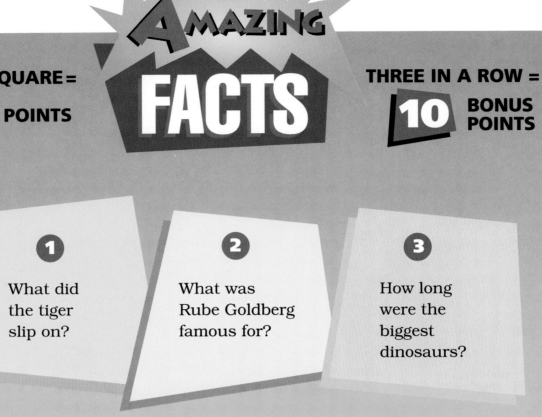

1 What did the tiger slip on?

2 What was Rube Goldberg famous for?

3 How long were the biggest dinosaurs?

4 Where do we hear an operator talk?

5 What kinds of animals were dinosaurs?

6 Jim Abbott has only one hand, but he played what sport?

7 How many cells are there in an adult body?

8 What was the old woman picking in her garden?

9 How much did the biggest dinosaurs weigh?

Harvest Figures

Come Into My Cave

The Stone Age

The Land I Lost

67

Art | Math | Music
Science | Social Studies
LANGUAGE ARTS

You can find the day of the week in any year from 1753 through 2030!

First: Under *Years,* find the year you're interested in and note the letter that follows it.

Second: Under *Months,* find the same letter, and note which number falls under the month you're looking for.

Third: Under *The Seven Calendars,* use the calendar under the number you have just found.

Years

	1786G	1821A	1856I	1891D	1926E	1961G	1996H
	1787A	1822B	1857D	1892L	1927F	1962A	1997C
1753A	1788I	1823C	1858E	1893G	1928N	1963B	1998D
1754B	1789D	1824K	1859F	1894A	1929B	1964J	1999E
1755C	1790E	1825F	1860N	1895B	1930C	1965E	2000M
1756K	1791F	1826G	1861B	1896J	1931D	1966F	2001A
1757F	1792N	1827A	1862C	1897E	1932L	1967G	2002B
1758G	1793B	1828I	1863D	1898F	1933G	1968H	2003C
1759A	1794C	1829D	1864L	1899G	1934A	1969C	2004K
1760I	1795D	1830E	1865G	1900A	1935B	1970D	2005F
1761D	1796L	1831F	1866A	1901B	1936J	1971E	2006G
1762E	1797G	1832N	1867B	1902C	1937E	1972M	2007A
1763F	1798A	1833B	1868J	1903D	1938F	1973A	2008I
1764N	1799B	1834C	1869E	1904L	1939G	1974B	2009D
1765B	1800C	1835D	1870F	1905G	1940H	1975C	2010E
1766C	1801D	1836L	1871G	1906A	1941C	1976K	2011F
1767D	1802E	1837G	1872H	1907B	1942D	1977F	2012N
1768L	1803F	1838A	1873C	1908J	1943E	1978G	2013B
1769G	1804N	1839B	1874D	1909E	1944M	1979A	2014C
1770A	1805B	1840J	1875E	1910F	1945A	1980I	2015D
1771B	1806C	1841E	1876M	1911G	1946B	1981D	2016L
1772J	1807D	1842F	1877A	1912H	1947C	1982E	2017G
1773E	1808L	1843G	1878B	1913C	1948K	1983F	2018A
1774F	1809G	1844H	1879C	1914D	1949F	1984N	2019B
1775G	1810A	1845C	1880K	1915E	1950G	1985B	2020J
1776H	1811B	1846D	1881F	1916M	1951A	1986C	2021E
1777C	1812J	1847E	1882G	1917A	1952I	1987D	2022F
1778D	1813E	1848M	1883A	1918B	1953D	1988L	2023G
1779E	1814F	1849A	1884I	1919C	1954E	1989G	2024H
1780M	1815G	1850B	1885D	1920K	1955F	1990A	2025C
1781A	1816H	1851C	1886E	1921F	1956N	1991B	2026D
1782B	1817C	1852K	1887F	1922G	1957B	1992J	2027E
1783C	1818D	1853F	1888N	1923A	1958C	1993E	2028M
1784K	1819E	1854G	1889B	1924I	1959D	1994F	2029A
1785F	1820M	1855A	1890C	1925D	1960L	1995G	2030B

Months

	January	February	March	April	May	June	July	August	September	October	November	December
A	1	4	4	7	2	5	7	3	6	1	4	6
B	2	5	5	1	3	6	1	4	7	2	5	7
C	3	6	6	2	4	7	2	5	1	3	6	1
D	4	7	7	3	5	1	3	6	2	4	7	2
E	5	1	1	4	6	2	4	7	3	5	1	3
F	6	2	2	5	7	3	5	1	4	6	2	4
G	7	3	3	6	1	4	6	2	5	7	3	5
H	1	4	5	1	3	6	1	4	7	2	5	7
I	2	5	6	2	4	7	2	5	1	3	6	1
J	3	6	7	3	5	1	3	6	2	4	7	2
K	4	7	1	4	6	2	4	7	3	5	1	3
L	5	1	2	5	7	3	5	1	4	6	2	4
M	6	2	3	6	1	4	6	2	5	7	3	5
N	7	3	4	7	2	5	7	3	6	1	4	6

The Seven Calendars

Days	1	2	3	4	5	6	7
Monday	1						
Tuesday	2	1					
Wednesday	3	2	1				
Thursday	4	3	2	1			
Friday	5	4	3	2	1		
Saturday	6	5	4	3	2	1	
Sunday	7	6	5	4	3	2	1
Monday	8	7	6	5	4	3	2
Tuesday	9	8	7	6	5	4	3
Wednesday	10	9	8	7	6	5	4
Thursday	11	10	9	8	7	6	5
Friday	12	11	10	9	8	7	6
Saturday	13	12	11	10	9	8	7
Sunday	14	13	12	11	10	9	8
Monday	15	14	13	12	11	10	9
Tuesday	16	15	14	13	12	11	10
Wednesday	17	16	15	14	13	12	11
Thursday	18	17	16	15	14	13	12
Friday	19	18	17	16	15	14	13
Saturday	20	19	18	17	16	15	14
Sunday	21	20	19	18	17	16	15
Monday	22	21	20	19	18	17	16
Tuesday	23	22	21	20	19	18	17
Wednesday	24	23	22	21	20	19	18
Thursday	25	24	23	22	21	20	19
Friday	26	25	24	23	22	21	20
Saturday	27	26	25	24	23	22	21
Sunday	28	27	26	25	24	23	22
Monday	29	28	27	26	25	24	23
Tuesday	30	29	28	27	26	25	24
Wednesday	31	30	29	28	27	26	25
Thursday		31	30	29	28	27	26
Friday			31	30	29	28	27
Saturday				31	30	29	28
Sunday					31	30	29
Monday						31	30
Tuesday							31

Make a Harvest Figure

Many cultures measure time by the harvest seasons. Harvest figures are made all over the world. In West Africa, they are made from bundles of grass. In Mexico, they are made from corn husks.

1. Fold a long piece of husk in half and stuff some cotton in the fold. Tie string around the husk to make a neck and head.

2. Roll up another husk for both arms. Tie each end to make hands. Slide the arm husk up under the first husk to the neck.

3. Stuff more cotton in the torso and tie it with string at the waist.

4. Arrange some husks around the waist and tie them in place.

5. *To make a girl figure:* Fold the loose ends down and trim straight across to make a skirt.

   To make a boy figure: Divide or cut the loose husks into two parts. Tie them at the ankles to make pant legs.

6. Draw or paint a face on your harvest figure and take it home.

THE TOLTECS

A POEM FROM ANCIENT MEXICO

The Toltecs were wise
they conversed with their own hearts

they played their drums
they played their rattles
they were singers
they made songs
the Toltecs guarded the songs
in their memories

the Toltecs were wise
they conversed with their own hearts

A

Vowel plus y = ys		Consonant plus y = ies		f or fe = ves	
day	days	baby	babies	calf	calves
key	keys	story	stories	half	halves
boy	boys	library	libraries	knife	knives
monkey	monkeys	candy	candies	wife	wives

o = os or oes		words that don't follow the rules			
tomato	tomatoes	child	children	man	men
potato	potatoes	foot	feet	woman	women
piano	pianos	tooth	teeth	mouse	mice
radio	radios	goose	geese	fish	fish

*Work with your partner. Take turns asking and answering the questions. Begin your answers with There **was** or There **were**.*

1. How many monkeys were in the zoo?
2. How many lions were there?
3. How many geese were there?
4. How many boys were there?
5. How many women were there?
6. How many children were there?

AMAZING FACTS

- Mazateco Indian men and women could hold a conversation just by whistling.

- Children of the Pueblo people ate corn at every meal. Popcorn was a treat long before Europeans came.

- About 300 years ago, toothbrushes were made from hog's bristles.

Ali Baba and the Forty Thieves

Once upon a time, there was a man named Ali Baba. Ali Baba was such a poor man that he had only one shoe for his two feet. Even the mice in his house were hungry.

One day, his wife said, "We have no food in the house. No rice. No potatoes. Go and collect leaves in the forest so that I can make a soup."

Ali was a lazy man. He looked for leaves for about ten minutes, and then he climbed a tree to sleep. He was afraid of wolves. When he woke up, he was surprised to see forty thieves on forty horses. They stopped in front of a big rock.

"Open Sesame!" shouted the leader. A door in the rock opened. The thieves carried sacks full of gold into the cave. When they had finished, the leader shouted, "Close Sesame!" and the door closed. As soon as the thieves had disappeared, Ali Baba jumped down from the tree, said, "Open Sesame," and went into the cave.

There were shelves all around the walls. The shelves were full of sacks. The sacks were full of gold. Ali took a sack home with him.

Unfortunately, one of the thieves saw Ali's footprints in the sand. He followed them to Ali's home. He took out his knife and made a cross on the door.

"Now I shall know which house it is," he said.

He rode off to get the other thieves. But Ali had seen the thief.

He and his wife took brooms and swept away the footprints. Then he made crosses on every door on the street. When the forty thieves arrived, they had their knives between their teeth. But they never found Ali—or the gold. And Ali and his wife lived happily ever after.

THE CAVE PEOPLE - LONG LONG AGO

Indian petroglyphs at Newspaper Rock, Utah

The Stone Age began over two and a half million years ago. People didn't even know how to read or write then. They used stones for tools and weapons. By the Ice Age, about 2 million years ago, people's lives had improved. For one thing, they had better tools. They had spears and harpoons and scrapers and knives. For another thing, they lived in caves in the region that is on the borders of what is now France and Spain. They were not very good housekeepers. They left everything they did not want on the floors of the caves. Over thousands of years, the garbage piled up and filled the caves.

During the last part of the Ice Age, people began drawing pictures on the walls of the caves. They showed the animals they hunted – the bison, the bear, the wild boar, the mammoth, and the rhinoceros. You could call the cave paintings the first neighborhood newspapers.

AMAZING FACTS

- The Chinese people invented the wheelbarrow over 2,000 years ago.
- Early humans invented the sewing needle over 20,000 years ago.

Just Joking

Where does a ten thousand pound dinosaur sleep?

Anywhere it wants

Art Math Music
Science Social Studies
LANGUAGE ARTS

DIGGING UP DIRT

Scientists learn a lot about humans of long ago by studying their garbage heaps. They've found berries and nuts nearly half a million years old!

DOG FINDS CAVE ART

A dog discovered caves of prehistoric art in France in 1940. The dog fell through a hole in the ground. Boys heard the dog barking for help. They saw the pictures when they rescued him.

Spelunker Adventure

Would you like to travel through an ancient cave? Then you would be called a spelunker. Spelunkers explore and make maps of caves. It's fun, but also dangerous. Spelunkers wear hard hats and head lamps and heavy clothes to protect themselves.

WHAT MAKES A CAVE?

Most caves are formed by water. The water seeps into the earth's surface and slowly starts dissolving the hard rock underground. It takes thousands of years for this kind of cave to form.

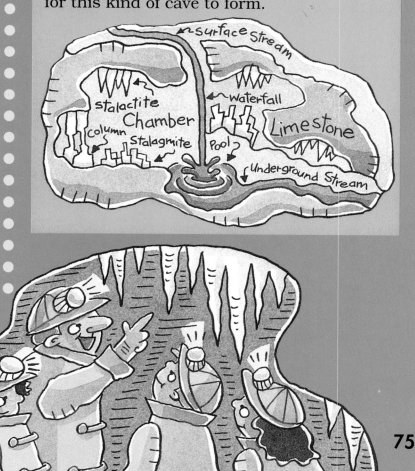

surface stream

stalactite

Chamber

column

Stalagmite

waterfall

Limestone

Pool

Underground Stream

A

keep	keeps	kept	leave	leaves	left
say	says	said	think	thinks	thought
build	builds	built	feel	feels	felt
send	sends	sent	sink	sinks	sank

Take turns with your partner. Read the sentences aloud and choose the right form of the verb.

1. My father (feel, feels) great today.
2. I (leaves, leave) for school at 8.
3. "Hey!" the officer (say, said).
4. Does the farmer (keep, keeps) pigs?
5. I (feels, feel) just so so today.
6. My mom (sleep, sleeps) late on Sunday.
7. Yesterday he (feels, felt) sick.
8. Did you (build, built) that house?
9. When did he (find, found) the money?
10. Did you (thought, think) about me?
11. Did they (left, leave) late?
12. What did you (thought, think) about?

The Three Wishes

Don, Wayne, and Warren were shipwrecked. Their ship sank in the Pacific Ocean. They found themselves on a desert island. They built a small hut and slept inside. They found food and water. They thought, "We'll be rescued soon."

But they weren't rescued. They left messages in the sand. They sent messages in bottles. Still, they weren't rescued. "Don't worry," Don said to his friends. But they felt worse and worse. They all thought about going home.

One day, Wayne found another bottle on the beach. He rubbed sand off of it—and a genie jumped out! "Oh, what a relief!" the genie said. "I have been captive in that bottle for 10,000 years. Now that I am free, I will give you three wishes."

"That means we can have one wish each," Warren said. "Well, I wish to be sent home immediately."

"Your wish is my command," said the genie. He waved his hand, and Warren disappeared.

"Wow! I want the same wish," said Wayne. "Your wish is my command," said the genie. And Wayne disappeared.

"Your turn," the genie said to Don.

"Gee, I'm not sure," Don answered. "Suddenly I felt so lonely without Wayne and Warren. I wish they were here to talk to."

"Your wish is my command," said the genie.

True or False?

1. Four men were shipwrecked.
2. Their ship sank in the Atlantic.
3. They built a hotel.
4. They thought they'd be rescued.
5. They left messages in the sand.
6. They sent messages by airmail.
7. Don found the bottle on the beach.
8. A genie jumped out of the bottle.
9. He gave the men three wishes.
10. All the men were sent home.

Guadalupe Perez works for a travel agency. She is a tour guide. She has been to Europe more than twenty times. Our *Amazing English* **Reporter** is interviewing her.

AER: What's your favorite tour, Ms. Perez?

P: That's hard to say. I like the tours in France. I like the tours through Italy and Germany, too.

AER: What do you have to do on a tour?

P: First, I meet everybody at the airport. I get all the tourists and their bags on the bus. Then I take them to their hotel.

AER: Then can you relax?

P: Oh, no. I'm in charge of every day on the tour. I get the tourists on the bus. I describe the sights. I make sure the meals are good. I help the tourists with their shopping.

If a tourist gets sick, I call a doctor. If a tourist gets lost, I have to find him or her.

AER: So you're busy twenty-four hours a day?

P: Just about. But I love my job.

AER: What languages do you speak, Guadalupe?

P: Well, Spanish and English, of course. I also speak French fairly well.

AER: It sounds like you are happy in your career.

P: I'm very happy. If you like people, and if you like to travel, being a tour guide is the best!

1. Work with your partner. Choose a place to visit in the United States. Research this place. What is there to see? What is there to do? What is it like to live there? Plan when to go, how to go, how long to stay, and how much money you'll need for your trip. Make an oral report.

2. Pretend you have taken your trip. Keep a diary of what you did every day. Did you meet any interesting people? Did you get lost? What was the best thing that happened? What was the worst thing?

3. Work with your partner. Choose any place in the world to visit. Research this place the same way you researched the place in the United States.

4. Work on your own. Find out where these famous things or places are: the Eiffel Tower, the Great Wall, the Hermitage, Tikal, Niagara Falls, Mt. Everest, the Kennedy Space Center, the Nile, the Parthenon, EPCOT Center.

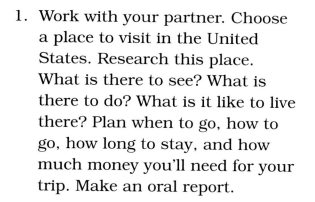

Dear Themework,
My partner and I chose Rio to visit. Seven beautiful beaches are in Rio de Janeiro, Brazil. The weather is great all year round. People from Brazil speak Portuguese. This is interesting, because the rest of the people in Latin America speak Spanish. This is a photo of Rio and the famous Sugarloaf Mountain.

Best,
Alia Sharif

The Land I Lost

EXCERPTED FROM THE BOOK
BY HUYNH QUANG NHUONG

I was born in the central highlands of Vietnam. Our small hamlet was on a riverbank that had a deep jungle on one side and a chain of high mountains on the other. Across the river, rice fields stretched to the slopes of another chain of mountains.

There were fifty houses in our hamlet. The houses were made of bamboo and covered with coconut leaves. Each was surrounded by a deep trench to protect it from wild animals or thieves. The only way to enter the house was to walk across a "monkey bridge." That was a single, bamboo stick. At night, we pulled the bridges into our houses and were safe.

There were no shops or marketplaces in our hamlet. If we needed supplies—medicine, cloth, soap, candles—we had to cross over the mountains to a town nearby.

During the six-month rainy season, nearly all of us helped to plant and cultivate crops. We grew rice, sweet potatoes, Indian mustard, eggplant, tomatoes, hot pepper, and corn. During the dry season, we became hunters and turned to the jungle. Wild animals played a very large part in our lives. There were four animals we feared most: the tiger, the wild hog, the crocodile, and the horse snake.

Like all farmers' children, I started working at the age of six. My seven sisters helped by working in the kitchen, gathering eggs, or taking water to the cattle. I looked after our herd of water buffaloes. I fished for the family, too.

My father was a farmer and a hunter, but he had a college education. In the evenings, he helped to teach other children in the hamlet. It was too small to afford a professional teacher.

My mother managed the house. During the harvest season, she could be found in the fields, helping my father. As the wife of a hunter, she knew how to dress and nurse a wound. She took good care of her husband and his hunting dogs.

I went to the lowlands to study for a while. I wanted to follow my father as a teacher when I grew up. I always planned to return to my hamlet to live the rest of my life there. But war disrupted my dreams. The land I love was lost to me forever.

Pioneer School

Many pioneer families moved to live west of the Mississippi River in the 1800s. The children went to schools that were different from your school.

▶ LISTEN

Listen to the beginning of the story. Then answer the questions.

1. Where did Roxana and her family live?
   a. in Virginia
   b. on a ranch in Texas
   c. on a farm in Kansas

2. What kept the schoolhouse warm?
   a. an oven
   b. a fireplace
   c. a cast-iron stove

3. What is sod?
   a. a tool
   b. hard-packed soil covered with grass
   c. a kind of soap

4. Why were many teachers so young?
   a. The pay was low, and many grown-ups had not been to school themselves.
   b. Teachers had to be strong.
   c. The ceilings in schoolhouses were low.

▶ SPEAK

Tell about what has happened so far. What chore do you think Roxana left unfinished?

▶ READ

Winter, 1869, 6 a.m.

Roxana was at the well. She was filling the bucket with water just as her brother Earl called to her.

"We have to leave now, or we'll be late for school. Hurry!" Roxana set the heavy bucket down and ran up to the house.

"Mama," she cried, "I have to go, or Earl will leave without me!" Before her mother could answer, Roxana grabbed her books and her lunch pail. She ran down the hill to catch up with Earl. Together they walked the two miles to school. When they got near the schoolhouse, they could hear the teacher ringing the big, iron bell to call them to class.

The students ranged in age from seven to seventeen years old. The teacher worked with one or two students around the same age at the same time. Older students often helped the younger ones. There was no special equipment of any kind—no textbooks, no maps, no posters, no bulletin boards, no videos, no cassette players, and no computers!

▶ WRITE

What do you think Roxana and Earl did after school?

▶ THINK

Do you think it would be hard or easy to learn in a one-room school? Why?

AMAZING FACTS

EACH SQUARE =
5 POINTS

THREE IN A ROW =
10 BONUS POINTS

1 Where is Rio de Janeiro?

2 Where did the Ice Age people draw pictures?

3 How far did Roxana and Earl have to walk to school?

4 How are caves formed?

5 What does Guadalupe Perez do in her career?

6 What four animals were the people in Vietnam afraid of?

7 What were toothbrushes made of about 300 years ago?

8 How did people enter the houses in the hamlet in Vietnam?

9 What do you call a person who explores caves?

Self Test Prep Portfolio
Traditional Performance
A S S E S S M E N T

Animals Around Us

Animal
Stickers

Animal
Talk

Butterflies

Rabbit
and Tiger

Suppose you were in charge of the circus train

1. What is the longest 2-car train you can make?
2. What is the shortest 2-car train you can make?
3. What are all the different lengths you can make for a train, using one engine and one or more other cars?

$2 \frac{1}{8}$ in. 3 in. $2 \frac{3}{4}$ in. $2 \frac{7}{8}$ in.

$2 \frac{1}{8}$ in. $2 \frac{1}{2}$ in. $1 \frac{3}{4}$ in. $2 \frac{7}{8}$ in.

3 in. $1 \frac{1}{4}$ in.

AMAZING FACTS

● Jean Damery of France built the smallest known working model railroad. His engine was only 5/16 of an inch long! On a scale of 1 : 1,000, a real engine would be how many feet long?

Animals Around Us

Art Math Music
Science Social Studies
LANGUAGE ARTS

Make Animal Stickers

Make your own animal stickers to decorate your favorite things.

YOU WILL NEED:

- plain paper
- ruler
- markers or crayons
- magazines for cutting pictures
- scissors

1. Use the ruler to draw a grid with six, nine, or twelve boxes.

2. Decide what animals you want on your stickers.
   Here are some suggestions:
   - animals that live on the same continent, like Africa or Australia
   - house pets
   - circus animals
   - farm animals
   - animals that lay eggs
   - any animals in order of size

3. Draw an animal in each square, or cut out pictures of animals and paste them in the squares. If you want, save room at the bottom of the square to write the name of the animal.

4. Cut out each square.

5. Put paste or glue on the back of the square when you're ready to decorate something.

6. Trade your stickers with your friends, or take them home and share them.

THE DOG AND THE BONE

One day, a dog was out taking a walk. He was carrying a bone in his mouth. As he was walking across a bridge, he looked down at the river.

The dog saw his own reflection in the water. But he thought it was another dog. "There's a dog looking up at me," he thought. "And he has a bone, too. That bone looks bigger than my bone. I'll frighten that dog and grab his bone away."

The dog began to bark. And, of course, as soon as he opened his mouth, he dropped his bone. It fell into the river and floated away. The dog had been very silly.

Don't be greedy for what others have.

A

Consonant plus y = ied	Vowel plus y = yed	Double consonants
try-tried	play-played	stop-stopped
cry-cried	enjoy-enjoyed	step-stepped
dry-dried	stay-stayed	beg-begged
hurry-hurried	employ-employed	jog-jogged
carry-carried		rip-ripped
bury-buried		
marry-married		

Look at the pictures. Work with your partner. Take turns asking and answering these questions.

1. Whom did the clown marry?

2. What did the dog bury?

3. What did the girl dry?

4. What did he play?

5. What did they enjoy?

6. Where did they stop?

MIRANDA AND MAX

Miranda and Max were leaving for the circus tour. They were stars in a chimpanzee act. One chimp named Charlie lived with Miranda and Max. Miranda packed their suitcases. Max packed Charlie's trunk; Charlie helped him. Max and Miranda carried the bags outside; Charlie helped them. Max walked back inside to call a taxi and check the house. Charlie helped him.

In the living room, the TV was playing. "Didn't I tell you to turn off the TV, Charlie?" said Max. Charlie turned off the TV. In the kitchen, Max noticed that the coffee pot was still plugged in. "Didn't I tell you to unplug the coffee pot, Charlie?" Charlie unplugged the coffee pot.

Max noticed that the back door was unlocked. "Didn't I tell you to lock the back door, Charlie?" Charlie locked the door. In the bathroom, the tub was full of water and Charlie's toys. "Didn't I tell you to empty the bathtub, Charlie?" said Max. Charlie emptied the bathtub. "And didn't I tell you to dry all your toys?" Charlie dried all the toys.

Finally, Max and Charlie walked back outside. "What have you been doing?" demanded Miranda. "And where is that taxi you called?"

"Taxi? Charlie, didn't I tell you to call a taxi?"

IT'S SHOCKING

The electric eel lives in rivers in South America. The front end of its body contains its brain and all of its major organs. The rest of the body is made up of tissue that generates an electric current. The power of an eel shock can knock a grown man off his feet. If you put an eel in salt water, however, it will short circuit itself!

Just Joking

Where do fish keep their money?

In the river bank!

AMAZING FACTS

- Grasshoppers are eaten in many parts of the world, including South America, Japan, Australia, and Africa. The arms and legs are removed before the bodies are fried!

- A snow leopard can jump 50 feet. The record for a human jump is 29 feet, 2 1/2 inches.

Butterfly Bites

The butterfly goes through a life cycle. First it is an egg; then it becomes a caterpillar. After that, it becomes a pupa and sleeps through the winter. Finally, it becomes a butterfly. The butterfly eats most when it is a caterpillar. It eats and eats until it bursts its skin and sheds it for a new one. This may happen many, many times until the caterpillar is much bigger than when it hatched from the egg.

And what is the favorite food of a butterfly? Nectar from flowers.

Animal Talk

When a male hippo opens his big, wide mouth, it may look like a yawn, but it's not. It's a warning to another hippo to clear out of his way–or be ready to fight. Hippos have excellent eyesight. When a hippo spots trouble, he grunts loudly.

A rhinoceros, on the other hand, has very poor eyesight. What a rhino can't see, he can smell and hear, however. A rhino may be looking the other way, but he still knows you're there. Instead of warning you by turning his head, he turns his whole body–fast–in your direction.

Bees don't see things the way we do, either. They see the world as flat areas of light and color. They communicate with each other by dancing! That's right. A bee will tell other bees it has found food by moving in figure eights. The center line of the bee's dance shows the direction the food is in. The length of the line shows how far away the food is.

Animals Around Us

A

take(s)	took	taken	break(s)	broke	broken
fall(s)	fell	fallen	tear(s)	tore	torn
throw(s)	threw	thrown	begin(s)	began	begun
know(s)	knew	known	swim(s)	swam	swum
go(es)	went	gone	see(s)	saw	seen

*Take turns with your partner. Read the sentences aloud
and choose the right form of the verb.*

1. ★ I (go, went) to the movies
   yesterday.
   ● What did you (saw, see)?
   ★ I (see, saw) *The Lion King.*
   ● Oh, I have already (saw, seen) it.

2. ★ Did you (went, go) to the beach
   last weekend?
   ● Yes, I (swim, swam) in the ocean.
   Then I (fell, fall) on some rocks,
   and I (tore, tear) my bathing suit.

3. ★ Janet (takes, took) the bus every
   day.
   ● Where does she (go, went)?
   ★ She (went, goes) to work at the zoo.

4. ★ I (take, took) a math test
   yesterday.
   ● Did you (knew, know)
   everything?
   ★ Of course not!

5. ★ Have you (saw, seen) my
   newspaper?
   ● I (threw, throw) it away.
   ★ But why?
   ● The dog (torn, tore) it up.

AMAZING FACTS

● Cows can smell
  odors 6 miles away.

● A giraffe sends food—
  about 75 pounds a
  day—down its long
  neck to one of its four
  stomachs.

● Fish don't have
  eyelids.

Mike and Bob went to the movies. It was a western. Outlaws had taken over a town.

The sheriff knew he needed help. He called a U.S. marshal. "Come as fast as you can," the sheriff said. The U.S. marshal began the long trip.

The outlaws were waiting for the marshal. They were hiding by the river. "I'll bet the marshal falls off his horse," said Mike.

"Nonsense," replied Bob. "He's the hero. I'll bet you he doesn't fall off." The two friends sat in silence for a few more minutes.

The marshal came to the river. The outlaws jumped out of their hiding place. The marshal's horse tripped and threw the marshal into the river. The marshal swam to shore and took cover behind a rock.

"I told you so!" Mike said.

"I can't believe it," Bob replied.

"Well, I have something to tell you," Mike said. "I have seen this movie before. I knew what was going to happen."

"Well, I have seen this movie before, too!" Bob said. "But I didn't think the marshal would be so stupid and fall off his horse again!"

Career Corner

Adam King has a very unusual job. He is the falconer at an Air Force base. A falconer trains falcons to hunt for other birds. Our *Amazing English* Reporter is interviewing him.

AER: Why does the Air Force need a falconer?

K: Because of bird strikes. That's when a large flock of birds fly into an airplane. A bird strike can damage engines. It's like throwing a rock at a car that's going over 100 miles per hour.

AER: But are bird strikes common?

K: Yes. Over 1,000 bird strikes at airports have been reported this year.

AER: Why do birds like airports?

K: Well, there is plenty of food in the open fields around an airport. And in the summer, after a heavy rain, thousands of worms crawl out onto the runways.

AER: Do the falcons kill the other birds?

K: No, we don't train them to kill. We train them to chase the other birds away.

AER How do you train your falcons?

K: Falcons will only do their job for food. After every flight, the falcon gets a mouse.

AER: How high do the falcons fly?

K: They patrol from about 3,000 feet. They can see any birds that try to fly over the airport.

AER: And how fast do the falcons fly?

K: In a dive, falcons can reach speeds of 120 miles per hour. It takes years to train a falcon. You can get very fond of them.

Art Math Music
Science Social Studies
LANGUAGE ARTS

1. Think about how animals help us. Make a chart with these headings:

Work	Clothing	Food	Entertainment

   Find out which animals belong in each list. Some may go under more than one heading. We eat the meat of sheep, for example. We also use their wool for clothing. Horses work on farms; they also entertain us in races, the circus, etc.

2. Make another chart with these headings:

Wild	Tame	Extinct

   Find out which animals belong in each list. Then choose one animal for a special report. Find out all you can about the animal. Organize your information for an oral report. Show pictures or make drawings.

3. Do you have a pet? Tell about it. Have you trained your pet to do any special tricks? If you don't have a pet, write and tell about a pet you'd like to have.

Dear Themework,
   I had a dog, but it died. For a long time, I was lonely for a pet. Then my dad took me to the Animal Shelter. I found the cutest puppy. He is gray now, but when he was a puppy, he was black. I trained him to take food only from my left hand. I trained him to roll over, to sit up, and to "wave" hello. My dog was a Christmas present, so I named him Chris Kringle.

Yours,
Kathy Sands

Animals Around Us

RABBIT AND TIGER
❖❖ A FOLKTALE FROM LATIN AMERICA ❖❖

(The Storyteller and the characters are on stage.)

Storyteller: Welcome to our play. Here are the characters.
Rabbit: Hi! I'm the Rabbit.
Tiger: Grr-ah! I'm the Tiger.
Farmer: And I'm the Farmer.

(The characters leave the stage.)

Storyteller: The Rabbit and the Tiger are not good friends.
Rabbit: *(pops out and laughs)* That's true!
Storyteller: That's because the Tiger is always trying to eat the Rabbit for breakfast, lunch, or dinner.
Tiger: *(pops out and growls)* That's not true!
Storyteller: But the rabbit is always too smart for the Tiger. One day, the Rabbit was sitting by a lake. *(Rabbit enters and sits.)* Soon, a Farmer came by. *(Farmer enters.)*

Art   Math   Music
Science   Social Studies
LANGUAGE ARTS

Farmer: Lah, Lah, lah, dee dah. Lah, lah. Oh, good morning, Rabbit.

Rabbit: Good morning, Farmer. What do you have there?

Farmer: I have some delicious cheese.

Rabbit: And where are you going with that cheese?

Farmer: I'm going to the market in town.

Rabbit: Hmm. Your cheese may spoil before you get there.

Farmer: Do you really think so?

Rabbit: Yes, I do really think so. Let me help you. I'll wrap your cheese in fresh, wet leaves.

Farmer: Well, that's very kind of you. *(The Rabbit leaves the stage and returns with some leaves.)*

Rabbit: Here you are. *(Rabbit gives the leaves to the Farmer.)*

Farmer: And here you are. *(The Farmer gives the Rabbit a nice big piece of cheese.)*

Rabbit: Thank you. That's very nice of you.

Farmer: I must go now. Good-bye. *(The Farmer leaves the stage.)*

Rabbit: Good-bye.

Storyteller: The Rabbit was enjoying his piece of cheese… when the Tiger came by. *(Tiger enters.)*

Tiger: Grr-ah! Now I have you! *(The Rabbit jumps up and pretends to be afraid.)* I'll eat you for lunch!

Rabbit: Well, first have a bite of this delicious cheese.

Tiger: *(Tiger tastes the cheese.)* Mmmmmm-mmm-gee-ah! Where did you get such delicious cheese?

Rabbit: *(pointing off stage)* From the bottom of the lake.

Tiger: *(surprised)* What? Cheese from the bottom of the lake?

Rabbit: Oh, yes. The lake is full of delicious cheese! The best cheese is at the bottom, of course. So I tied two stones to my tail.

Tiger: You tied two stones to your tail?

Rabbit: Yes. And then I jumped in and swam to the bottom.

Tiger: You jumped in and swam to the bottom?

Rabbit: Yes, and I got this delicious cheese.

Tiger: Well, then I will do just the same. *(Tiger exits.)*

Storyteller: As I said, the Rabbit is always too smart for the Tiger. What do you think happens next? *(Pause: Storyteller listens to the audience.)*

Storyteller: Well, this is what happened. The Tiger tied two stones to his tail. He swam to the bottom of the lake. The Rabbit laughed and laughed. As he was laughing, the Farmer came back. *(Farmer enters.)*

Farmer: Rabbit! Rabbit! I saw the Tiger heading this way.

Rabbit: I know. No problem.

Farmer: No problem?

Rabbit: Tiger is at the bottom of the lake.

Farmer: At the bottom of the lake? Whatever for?

Rabbit: For a piece of delicious cheese!

Farmer: For a piece of cheese? I don't understand.

Rabbit: Neither does the Tiger. Come on I'll explain. *(The Farmer and the Rabbit exit.)*

Storyteller: So the Farmer and the Rabbit went off together. They left the poor Tiger at the bottom of the lake. The Tiger nearly drowned, of course. And of course, he didn't find any cheese at the bottom of the lake. Here he comes now.

Tiger: *(sputtering, coughing, and shaking)* Rabbit! Rabbit! Where are you? *(sits and shakes his head)* Grrr-ah! Oh, double GRRR-AH! I'll find that Rabbit and have him for dinner if it's the last thing I do! *(curtain)*

LISTEN   SPEAK

A Man, His Son, and a Donkey

• •

Here is a picture of a man
and his wife, their son, and
their donkey. You will hear
about these people as you
listen to a folktale from
long ago.

▶ LISTEN

Listen to the beginning of the story. Then answer the questions.

1. Why did the man's wife want to
   sell the donkey?
   a. The donkey was too noisy.
   b. They needed more money.
   c. They wanted to buy a horse.

2. What did the friend tell the man
   he should do?
   a. Ask for many gold coins for
      the donkey.
   b. Take the donkey home and
      keep it.
   c. Let one of them ride the
      donkey to town.

3. What did the old man tell the man
   he should do?
   a. Let his son ride the donkey to
      town.
   b. Ride the donkey and have his
      son walk.
   c. Give the donkey a drink of
      water.

4. What did the old woman tell the
   man he should do?
   a. Let his son ride the donkey
      with him.
   b. Sing a song on the way to
      town.
   c. Send his son back home.

▶ SPEAK

Tell about what has happened so far. What advice do you
think the farmer will give the man? How will the man, his
son, and the donkey get to town?

Self Holistic Portfolio
Traditional Performance
A S S E S S M E N T

Theme 5

READ

The farmer said, "Are you crazy? Both of you are riding the donkey. The donkey won't make it to town. You should carry the donkey to town."

So the man and his son tied the donkey to a pole. They carried the donkey into town. The townspeople laughed and laughed. The noise frightened the donkey. He kicked himself off the pole and ran away.

"What are you going to tell mother?" the son asked.

"Well son," the man said, "I agreed to sell the donkey to please your mother. You rode the donkey to please my friend. I rode the donkey to please the old man. We both rode the donkey to please the old woman. We even carried the donkey to please the farmer!"

The man sighed. Then he said, "This is what I'm going to tell your mother. You can't please everybody. In the end, you please nobody, not even yourself."

WRITE

Do you think the man learned an important lesson? Explain your answer.

THINK

What else do you think the old man could do to earn money for his family?

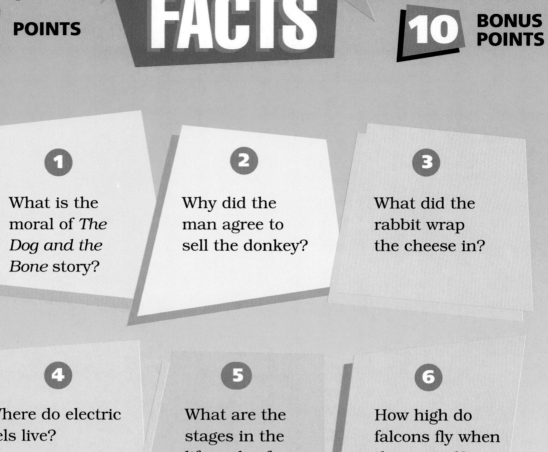

AMAZING FACTS

EACH SQUARE = **5** POINTS

THREE IN A ROW = **10** BONUS POINTS

1 What is the moral of *The Dog and the Bone* story?

2 Why did the man agree to sell the donkey?

3 What did the rabbit wrap the cheese in?

4 Where do electric eels live?

5 What are the stages in the life cycle of a butterfly?

6 How high do falcons fly when they patrol?

7 What is the favorite food of a butterfly?

8 Where did the tiger go to get cheese?

9 How do bees communicate?

Self Test Prep Portfolio
Traditional Performance
A S S E S S M E N T

Theme 5

Outdoor Adventures

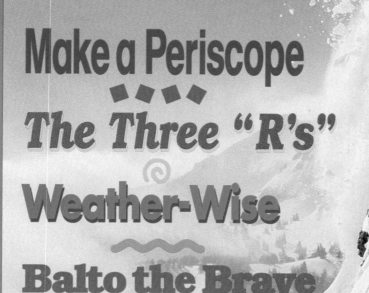

Make a Periscope

▶ ▶ ▶ ▶

The Three "R's"

@

Weather-Wise

〜〜〜

Balto the Brave

Art Math Music
Science Social Studies
LANGUAGE ARTS

Theme 6

There's going to be a road race next month. Here's the map. As a runner, you can follow either the roads or the paths. The roads are the black lines. The paths are the dotted lines.

You will start at A and finish at G. You must pass through Checkpoint C, but you can take any route you want after that. Find the fastest route! Be careful. One mile by path takes the same time as five miles by road.

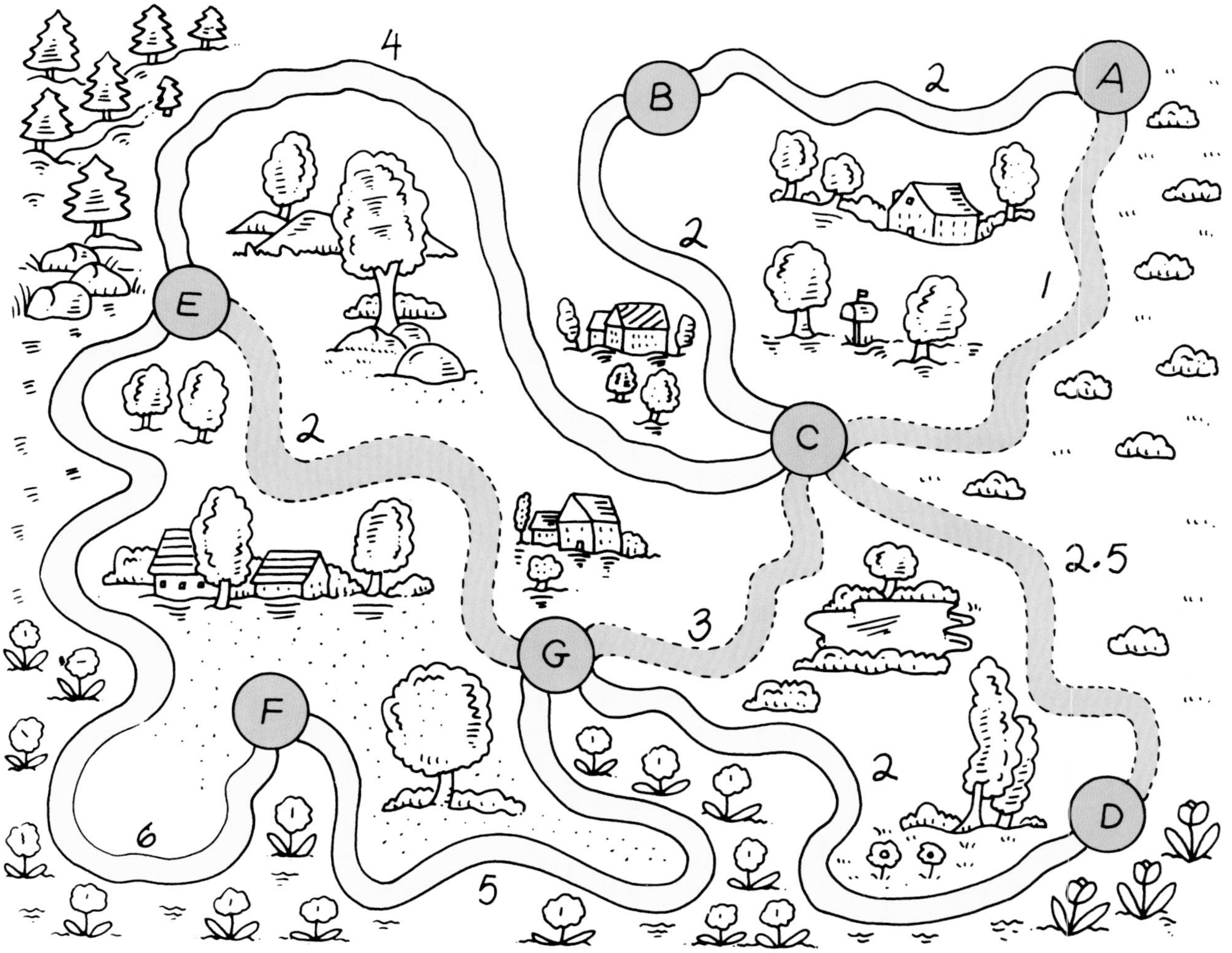

A - B - C - E - G = 18 miles by road. From A to C, the road (4 miles) is shorter than the path (equivalent to 5 miles).

C - E - F - G	4+6+5=15
C - G	3x5=15
C - D - G	(2.5x5) +2=14.5
C - E - G	4 + (2x5) =14

Make a Periscope

YOU WILL NEED:

- scissors
- a clean, empty milk carton
- two pocket-sized mirrors
- tape

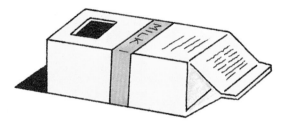

1. Cut a hole in one side of the carton about 1 inch from the top.

2. Cut a hole in the opposite side of the carton about 1 inch from the bottom.

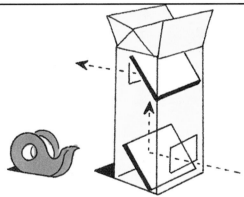

3. Open the top carefully. Tape the two mirrors inside. Tape them at a 45 degree angle.

4. Tape the top of the carton shut. Decorate your periscope.

5. Take your periscope to a corner. Hold it so just one hole is sticking out. Look through the other hole, and you'll be able to see around the corner!

THE WIND AND THE SUN

Once upon a time, the Wind and Sun got into an argument. The Wind said, "I'm stronger than you, Sun." The Sun said, "Nonsense. I am stronger than you, and I'll prove it. See that man down there? Let's see which one of us can make him take off his cape."

So the Wind blew and blew and blew. The man did not take off his cape. The Wind blew harder. The man wrapped his cape around him tighter. The Wind gave up and told the Sun to try.

The Sun began to smile. It grew warmer and warmer. The Sun shone brighter and brighter. The man felt very warm. The Sun shone as bright as it could. The man felt very hot and threw off his cape.

Gentleness can accomplish what force cannot.

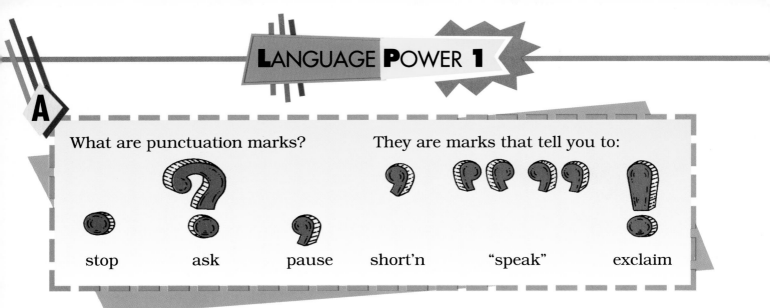

A

What are punctuation marks?   They are marks that tell you to:

stop   ask   pause   short'n   "speak"   exclaim

1. the **Period** ●
   When you come to the end of a
   thought,
   Sign off with this dot.

2. the **Question Mark** ?
   At the end of something you
   must ask,
   Make this mark your task.

3. the **Comma** ,
   A sentence is a band of words
   going for a walk.
   A comma is a pause for breath
   when you talk.
   And when you write,
   you use the comma because
   it gives your reader a
   chance to pause.

4. the **Apostrophe** ,
   An apostrophe shows who
   owns a thing,

Like Mary's hat, my sister's cat,
and a girl's ring.
An apostrophe also shrinks
words—do not into don't,
Have not to haven't and will
not to won't.

5. **Quotation Marks** " "
   They let you know who says
   what.
   A pair of marks is what you've
   got.
   "Wow!" said Ben.
   "What?" asked Tim.
   "No," replied Sally.

6. **Exclamation Point** !
   If you want to scare, command,
   or excite,
   It's the mark that you should
   write.

The Pirate Flag

Take turns reading the following story out loud with a partner. One of you should read the words. The other should read the punctuation marks. How? Just follow the simple code at the bottom of the page.

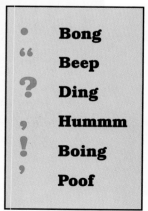

"What ho!" cried Pirate Pat, sitting in the crow's nest. "Thunder and lightning! There's a treasure ship. Look lively, my cutthroats!"

Pirate Pat slid down to the ship's deck.

"How far away is the ship?" asked Blackbeard, the pirate captain.

"We'll meet the ship before the sun sets," said Pirate Pat. "What are your orders, Captain?"

"Mates! Listen!" called Blackbeard. "Put up a false flag. Stay well hidden. When we're almost upon them, we'll raise our flag. Raise the pirate flag! That'll be a beautiful surprise, hey?" And Blackbeard laughed a deep, mean, nasty, chilling, scary, gruesome, eerie, wild, awful, terrifying, pirate laugh.

•	**Bong**
"	**Beep**
?	**Ding**
,	**Hummm**
!	**Boing**
,	**Poof**

TUNED IN TO WEATHER

*"When cows and sheep huddle by tree and bush,
Bad weather is coming with wind and slush."*

This Apache Indian saying tells what most farmers already know—domestic animals change their behavior when a storm is coming.

YOUR PETS CAN PREDICT WEATHER CHANGES, TOO.

- When a cat sneezes, it's a sign of rain.
- When dogs rub themselves in winter, it will thaw soon.
- When an old cat acts like a frisky kitten, a storm is on the way.
- Dogs' tails straighten when rain is near.
- If you see sparks when you stroke a cat's back, the weather will change soon.
- A dog rolling on the ground is a sign of violent wind.

AMAZING FACTS

When your trash goes to a landfill, it doesn't decompose right away. The list below gives you an idea of how long things last.

- Paper – 20-30 days
- Cloth – 6 months
- Wood – 4 years
- Tin – 12-15 years
- Plastic – 5,000 years
- Glass – forever

HURRICANE Names

You may have noticed that every time there's a hurricane, it's given a name – like Hurricane Bob. Why? In the early 1900s, Australian weatherman Clement Wraggle started naming hurricanes after people he didn't like. Today, the names of future hurricanes are chosen way in advance and in alphabetical order.

Just Joking

What would happen if you threw a yellow rock into the Red Sea?

It would get wet.

HOT & COLD

Here are the average temperatures in one of the coldest – and one of the hottest – cities in the USA. The temperatures are in degrees Fahrenheit.

	Jan/Feb	Mar/Apr	May/Jun	Jul/Aug	Sep/Oct	Nov/Dec
Juneau, Alaska	25	35	50	56	46	30
Miami, Florida	68	74	80	83	80	71

If you visited Juneau on your birthday, what would the temperature probably be? What would it be if you visited Miami?

That's A Lot Of Trash

Every day, the average person in the U.S. throws away more than three and a half pounds of trash. Every month, we throw out our own weight in packaging alone. Packaging includes the boxes, bags, wrappings, and labels that stuff comes in.

Where does all that trash go? Most of it ends up buried in a landfill, but the landfills in many cities in the U.S. are almost filled. Many of the old landfills contain poisonous substances that can make the water and soil around them dangerous to your health.

WHAT CAN YOU DO TO HELP?
Follow the three R's:
REUSE, REFUSE, and RECYCLE.

Reuse. You don't need new grocery bags every time you go to the store. Reuse the old ones—and use paper, not plastic.

Refuse. Stop buying stuff that is overpackaged. Also look for products that come in boxes made of recycled cardboard.

Recycle. Soda cans can be used again. Newspapers can be ground up and made into newsprint. Plastic bottles can be made into insulation for sleeping bags.

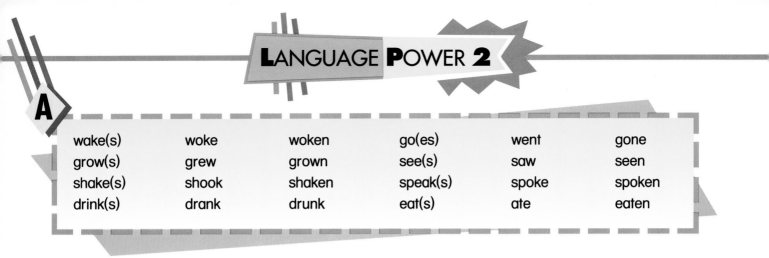

A

wake(s)	woke	woken	go(es)	went	gone
grow(s)	grew	grown	see(s)	saw	seen
shake(s)	shook	shaken	speak(s)	spoke	spoken
drink(s)	drank	drunk	eat(s)	ate	eaten

Work with your partner. Take turns asking and answering the questions.

1. ★ What time did you (woke, wake) up?
   ● I (wake, woke) up at eight.

2. ★ I (left, leave) home every day at 8:00.
   ● Did you (left, leave) yesterday at 8:00?
   ★ No, I (leaves, left) at 9:00 yesterday.
   ● Where did you (went, go)?
   ★ I (go, went) to the museum.

3. ★ Lou (wake, wakes) up every day at 6:00.
   ● Where does he (went, go) first?
   ★ He (gone, goes) to the kitchen.

4. ★ Have you ever (ate, eaten) snake?
   ● No, but I have (eat, eaten) octopus!

5. ★ Last year, we (grow, grew) tomatoes.
      We (eaten, ate) tomatoes every day.
      We (drunk, drank) tomato juice every day.
      We have all (grew, grown) tired of tomatoes.

AMAZING FACTS

- ● The Venus flytrap can snap shut on a bug in less than $\frac{1}{2}$ a second.

- ● The largest iceberg ever found in Antarctica was 208 miles long and 60 miles wide.

- ● Only one quart of oil can ruin 250,000 gallons of drinking water.

A Case of the Great Indoors

Lou woke up. He looked at the clock, turned over, and went back to sleep. The alarm woke him up again. Still he didn't get up.

Lou's mother saw her son still asleep in bed. She shook him by the shoulders. "Come on, Lou. Time to get ready for school."

"I don't want to go!" Lou said. "I can't stand the thought of school."

"Now, Lou. We both know you have to go. I have grown tired of telling you that every day. Now get up!" Lou finally got up.

Later, after Lou had eaten his breakfast, his mother spoke to him again. "You'll be late, Lou. Have you seen what time it is?"

" I don't care if I'm late. I don't care if I never go to school again!"

"Son, you know as well as I do—you have to go."

"Give me two good reasons," Lou said.

"First, you are forty-two years old. And second, you're the principal!"

Rose Bush is an expert on plants and the environment. Our **Amazing English Reporter** is interviewing her at an experimental greenhouse.

AER: I understand that many trees are dying.

B: That's right. There's a huge amount of pollution in the air. Pollution kills trees, plants, even animals.

AER: Where does the pollution come from?

B: Well, some of it comes from factories. Some of it comes from cars and trucks.

AER: How does pollution spread?

B: The wind carries it. It spreads it far away from the place where it began. When it rains, the pollution in the air comes back down. We call that acid rain.

AER: Why is acid rain a bad thing?

B: Acid rain is killing whole forests. It's poisoning the soil. It's poisoning our lakes and rivers.

AER: Is acid rain really a serious problem?

B: Absolutely. Some scientists believe that in twenty years all the great forests of the world may be dead.

Art | Math | Music
Science | Social Studies
LANGUAGE ARTS

1. Make a chart of traffic patterns in your town or city. First, list all the different vehicles you can think of. Then stand on a corner and check all of the vehicles that pass in 15 minutes. Do this at different times on different days, if you can. When was there the most traffic? When was there the least traffic? What kinds of pollution did you see?

2. Find out more about acid rain. Find out more about how we get rid of garbage. . .not just ordinary garbage, but dangerous garbage. This kind of garbage is called toxic waste.

3. Did you know that many things in your home can be dangerous to your health?

Products like oven cleaner, drain cleaner, paint, bug sprays—even furniture polish—can be dangerous. You can find out more by writing the Sierra Club. Your teacher has the address.

Dear Themework,
    A bunch of us made a chart on traffic patterns in front of our school. In the morning, the traffic was terrible. We counted 643 cars, trucks, and buses in just fifteen minutes! We were really busy. And the air was terrible. Now I know why the trees are dying.

    Yours truly,
    Frank Hogan

Outdoor Adventures

Balto the Brave

A TRUE STORY FROM ALASKA

Balto was the lead dog on a team of sled dogs. His owner's name was Gunnar. Gunnar thought that Balto was the smartest and bravest dog in Alaska.

In January 1925, Nome, Alaska, was buried in snow. People were sick with diphtheria. They needed medicine from the hospital in Anchorage. Doctors in Anchorage put the medicine on a train, but the train derailed in a terrible snow storm. The medicine was still 700 frozen miles from Nome.

Art   Math   Music
Science   Social Studies
LANGUAGE ARTS

The mayor of Nome radioed for help. "We need the best men and the best sled dogs in the area. We'll work in relay teams. We must get the medicine here as soon as possible. It's a matter of life and death for the people of Nome."

Gunnar volunteered right away. Twenty other men with dog sleds volunteered, too. Gunnar's place in the relay was at Bluff. Gunnar and Balto waited for the sled team from Golowin.

The first sled driver reached the train. He wrapped the medicine in fur to keep it from freezing and raced to the next stop in the relay route. The medicine was still 400 frozen miles from Nome.

The storm grew worse. Two dogs on one team froze in the snow. The driver of the team took their place and hitched himself to the sled. The medicine was still 200 frozen miles from Nome.

Many more men and dogs struggled through the storm. Finally, the sled from Golowin reached Bluff. "Mush – go!" shouted Gunnar. Balto leaped into the dark night. The medicine was still 53 frozen miles from Nome.

The storm grew even worse. The sled dogs sank in the snow and began to panic. But Balto led his team on. At last, they reached Point Safety, but there was no relay team waiting! Gunnar and Balto didn't even slow down. The medicine was still 31 frozen miles from Nome.

Just before dawn, the team reached Nome. They had fought through 53 frozen miles without stopping. The medicine was finally in Nome.

"You're a hero," the Mayor said to Gunnar. "No, Balto is the hero," said Gunnar. "Balto is the smartest and bravest dog in all of Alaska."

The Mole and the Water Rat

• • • • • • • • • • • • • • • • • • • •

The Wind in the Willows is a famous book. Here is a story about how two characters from that book, the Mole and the Water Rat, become friends.

▶ LISTEN

Listen to the beginning of the story. Then answer the questions.

1. How do you know what time of year it is?
   a. Mole was tired and his back ached.
   b. Mole was spring-cleaning his house.
   c. Mole climbed up, up, up.

2. What had Mole never seen before?
   a. a river
   b. the sunshine
   c. a field

3. How did the Water Rat get across the river?
   a. He called to Mole in a friendly voice.
   b. He walked over a bridge.
   c. He rowed across in a little blue and white boat.

4. Where did the two animals agree to go?
   a. They wanted to sit on the grassy bank.
   b. They decided to go down the river together.
   c. They went back to Mole's house.

▶ SPEAK

Tell about what has happened so far. What do you think Mole and the Water Rat saw on their trip down the river?

Self Holistic Portfolio
Traditional Performance
A S S E S S M E N T

READ

The Water Rat fetched a wicker picnic basket. "Shove that under your feet," he said to the Mole. The Mole settled back on the soft cushions, and Ratty rowed silently down the river. Mole took in all the new sights, smells and sounds of the river. Soon they came to a nice place for their picnic.

While they were eating, they met two of Ratty's friends—the Otter and the Badger. Mr. Toad was on the river, too. He shot by in a new racing boat. He was short and fat, splashing badly, and rolling from side to side. "Toad's always trying something new," explained Rat. "Last year, he had a houseboat. But he soon gets tired of things."

The Rat and the Mole went back to Rat's snug home in the River Bank. They sat in armchairs beside a bright fire, chatting away. Rat invited Mole to stay with him for the summer. The happy Mole went to sleep in a comfy bedroom. His new friend, the River, was lapping against the bank. And he could hear the wind, whispering in the willows.

WRITE

What other adventures do you think Mole and Ratty had during the summer? Write about some of them.

THINK

Why did Mole want to stay with the Water Rat for the summer?

AMAZING FACTS

EACH SQUARE =
5 POINTS

THREE IN A ROW =
10 BONUS POINTS

1 What does pollution come from?

2 What do domestic animals do when a storm is coming?

3 What sickness did the people in Nome, Alaska, have?

4 What did weatherman Clement Wraggle do for hurricanes?

5 What punctuation mark shows who owns something?

6 Where does most trash go?

7 How did the medicine get to Nome, Alaska?

8 What is acid rain?

9 What are the three R's for helping to make less trash?

Self | Test Prep | Portfolio
Traditional | Performance
ASSESSMENT

INDEX

A Publication of the World Language Division

Director of Product Development: Judith M. Bittinger
Executive Editor: Elinor Chamas
Editorial Development: Kathleen M. Smith
Text and Cover Design: Taurins Design Associates
Art Direction and Production: Taurins Design Associates
Production and Manufacturing: James W. Gibbons

Cover Art: Diane Harris

Illustrators: Teresa Anderko 4, 25, 109; Donna Ayers 104,105, 124, 125; Don Baker 8, 28, 46 top, 50, 72, 77, 96, 97; Doron Ben-Ami 56, 57, 78; Lee Lee Brazeal 91; Chi Chung 16-19, 73, 100-103; Vo Dinh-Mai 80-83; Mena Dolobowsky 5, 112; Eldon Doty 49; David Frampton 42, 43, 111; Annie Gusman 89, 116; Diane Harris 29, 58, 59, 60, 61, 62, 63, 92, 113; Meryl Henderson 24, 88, 108; Amy Hill 7; Gay Holland 120-123; Joy Keenan 85; Susan Lexa 47, 68; Karen Loccisano 12, 13, 51, 54, 76; Sara Love 71; Elizabeth Miles 64; Sue Miller 24, 46; Brenda Mishell (handwriting) 15, 57, 79, 99, 119; Cyd Moore 9, 27, 117; Deborah Pinkney 78, 119 top; Chris Reed 6, 26, 48, 70, 90, 110; Roger Roth 32,33; Jackie Snider 10-11, 75, 94-95, 114-115; David Tamura 20, 21; Debbie Tilley 93.

Photographs: Allied Artists, Bad Men of Tombstone 97; Bellevue School District 11; Kathleen Sands Boehmer 99; Bettman Archive 31; Gary Braasch/Woodfin Camp 3; Dominique Braud 87; D. Donne Bryant/Picture Perfect USA 74; J. Chenet/Woodfin Camp 115; Gregory G. Dimijian/Photo Researchers 95; Eastcott, Momatiuk/The Image Works 35; Bud Fawcett/Mountain Stock 107; Robert Frerck/Woodfin Camp 34, 67; George Holton/Photo Researchers 79; Kansas State Historical Society 84; Stephanie Maze/Woodfin Camp 23; Murphy Library, University of Wisconsin—LaCrosse 14; © Photo File Inc., Elmsford NY 10523, pp. 45, 52; H. Rogers/Monkmeyer 118.

Acknowledgements: Page 6, "Math Slat Book," from *Multicultural Books To Make And Share* by Susan Gaylord. Copyright © 1993 by Scholastic Inc. Reprinted by permission. Pages 36-41, "Family Pictures" from *Family Pictures* Copyright © 1990 Carmen Lomas Garza, published by Children's Book Press, San Francisco. Page 49, "The Meal," from *Dogs and Dragons, Trees and Dreams*, by Karla Kuskin, Copyright © 1962 by Karla Kuskin. Page 53, "Back Scratcher," reprinted with special permission of King Features Syndicate, by Rube Goldberg. Page 71, "The Toltecs," from *2-Rabbit, 7-Wind*, Copyright © 1971 by Toni de Gerez. Pages 80-83, Abridged excerpt from *The Land I Lost*, by Huynh Quang Nhuong. Copyright © 1982 by Huynh Quang Nhuong.